David
Lincoln
Aug. '91

W9-BEE-707

Washington Irving

Columbus

The Voyage of 1492

About the editor.

Francisco Pabón Flores, Ph.D, is Associate Professor of American Studies at the State University of New York at Buffalo since 1969. He makes his home away from home in Granada at the foot of the Alhambra.

Book Design & Typesetting by Camilo Pabón.
Set in New Baskerville and Drop Caps.
Copyright © 1989 Francisco Pabón Flores.
All Rights Reserved.
Printed in Spain at Imprenta La Gráfica, Granada.
Bound by Encuadernaciones Olmedo, Granada. Spain.
ISBN 84 - 404 - 5444 - 9
Depósito Legal GR 1222 - 1989

Contents

Prologue

Maps of 1492

1

2

3

4

Prologue

ashington Irving was born in New York City, April 3, 1783. By the time he went to Spain in 1826 he had made his mark as the most popular comic writer in America for three widely read books about New York— *The Letters of Jonathan Oldstyle, Gent* (1802), *Salmagundi* (1807-8) and *Diedrich Knickerbocker's History of New York from the Creation to the End of the Dutch Dynasty* (1809)— and then as the first American writer to achieve international acclaim for a bestseller in England, the U.S. and the Continent —*The Sketchbook of Geoffrey Crayon, Gent* (1819-20).

The United States was a new nation and American writers were unknown and unrecognized in the world of letters. The emergence of Irving as a writer of note at that time is a landmark in the history of American writing:

"In 1820 an irascible English aphorist, Sydney Smith, having suffered, as had many Europeans, just about all the American boasting he could stand, delivered a blast...The American Republic, Smith said, had nothing in the way of arts, manners, or intellect to show for itself: 'And who, the wide world over, reads an American book?' His jibe could hardly have been more ill timed, for even as he uttered it, a book was taking shape, Washington Irving's *The Sketch Book*, which everybody in America, just about everybody in Great Britain, and then thousands upon the Continent fell to reading with avidity...For the two years in which *The Sketch Book* was bit by bit appearing, Washington Irving made a profit of $9,000, which no other writer in England except Sir Walter Scott could come near, and none in America." (Perry Miller, *Afterword* to *The Sketch Book*, 1961).

Irving went to Spain to translate a book on Columbus that was being published by a noted Spanish historian, Martin Fernandez de Navarrete. Instead Irving produced the first popularized biography of Columbus written in English, *The Life and Voyages of Christopher Columbus* (1828). Irving documented the making of Columbus in letters he wrote to friends, family and his publisher:

"Since my arrival in Spain, I have principally been employed on my *Life of Columbus*, in executing which I have studied and labored with a patience and assiduity for which I shall never get the credit...There is an independent delight in study and in the creative exercise of the pen; we live in a world of dreams, but publication lets in the noisy rabble of the world, and there is an end to our dreaming...In the house of the American consul, Obadiah Rich, a great collector of books for the London market...I am surrounded by everything rare in Spanish literature. I had no idea of the literary wealth of the language...The work which I had intended to translate is a voluminous mess of mere documents...but which in their present form would repel the general class of readers... I had no idea of what a complete laby-rinth I had entangled myself in when I took hold of Columbus..."

Irving followed Columbus through the Spanish labyrinth of history and literature that linked the fall of the Moorish kingdom of Granada, the rise of the Catholic Kings, and the dawn of the Spanish Empire in the New World. From 1826 to 1829 Irving lived and wrote in Spain, mostly in Madrid, Seville and Granada, and traversed the country from north to south and east to west. In quick succession he produced *The Life and Voyages of Christopher Columbus* (1828), *A Chronicle of the Conquest of Granada* (1829), *The Companions of Columbus* (1831), *and The Alhambra* (1832). These works established Irving as the first in a line of distinguished popularizers of Spain in English that include Prescott, Hemingway, Brennan, Orwell and Michener. *The Alhambra* became a classic and is still a memorable romantic sketch of Moorish Spain.

In 1832 Irving returned to New York, explored the West, and wrote *A Tour of the Prairies* (1835), *Astoria* (1836) and *The Adventures of Captain Bonneville* (1837). In 1842 Irving went back to Madrid and until 1846 served as U.S. Minister to Spain during the turbulent regency and reign of the adolescent Queen Isabella II. Upon his final return to the United States Irving settled in his family home, Sunnyside on the Hudson River, and dedicated himself to writing major biographies: *Oliver Goldsmith* (1849), *Mahomet and his Successors* (1850), and *George Washington* (1855-1859) and to revising his writings for the Samuel Putnam edition of his works.

Irving died on November 28, 1859. A modern reading of his works reveals that Washington Irving fathered and fashioned the essential themes of the best American writing that flows through Mark Twain (the folk sketches, the river and the frontier, the quixotic adventures abroad), Henry James (the expatriate American writer in Europe, the ways, manners and language of high society), and Ernest Hemingway (the spirits and legends of Spain). In fact, Irving's extensive and rich collection of letters is in its own right one of the great bodies of correspondence in American literature. They reveal Irving as the first modern writer in America— intent and consistent in the pursuit of his craft and business as a writer, planning and marketing his works, struggling to have the time, peace and resources to

write and produce books. A sample of his correspondence, nearly unknown to the general reading public
today, is now available in a special edition we have prepared entitled *The Spanish Letters of Washington Irving*
(1826—1829).

The Mediterranean Kingdoms of 1492

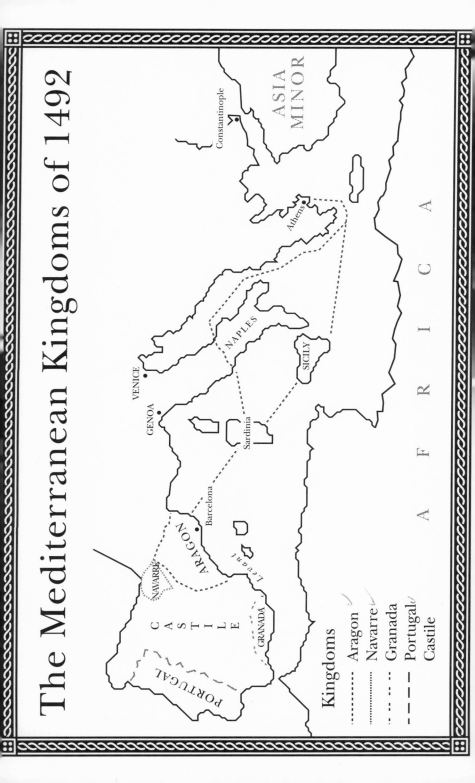

ASIA MINOR

Constantinople

A F R I C A

Athens

VENICE

GENOA

NAPLES

SICILY

Sardinia

Barcelona

ARAGON

NAVARRE

Levant

C
A
S
T
I
L
E

GRANADA

PORTUGAL

Kingdoms

.... Aragon
.... Navarre
.. — .. — Granada
— — — Portugal
Castile

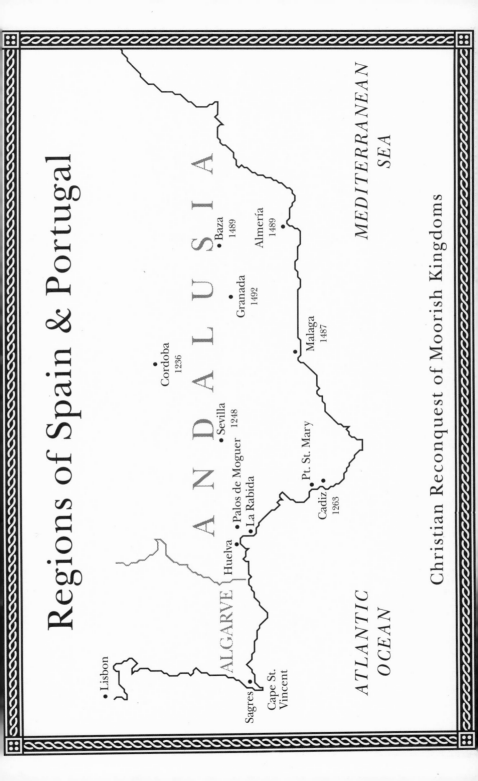

Regions of Spain & Portugal

ANDALUSIA

MEDITERRANEAN
SEA

- Baza
1489
- Almería
1489
- Granada
1492
- Malaga
1487
- Cordoba
1236
- Sevilla
1248
- Palos de Moguer
- La Rabida
- Huelva
ALGARVE
- Pt. St. Mary
- Cadiz
1263
- Lisbon
- Sagres
Cape St.
Vincent

ATLANTIC
OCEAN

Christian Reconquest of Moorish Kingdoms

The Known World in 1492

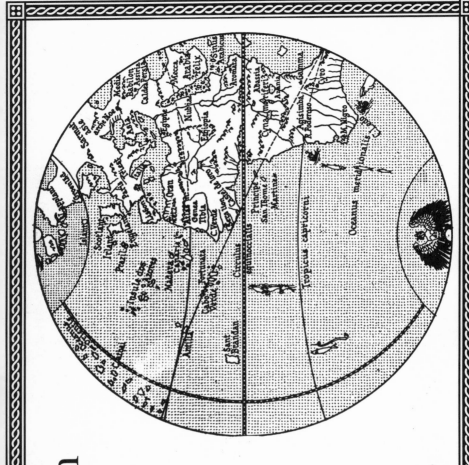

The globe made by
Martin Benhaim
a few months before
Columbus' discovery.

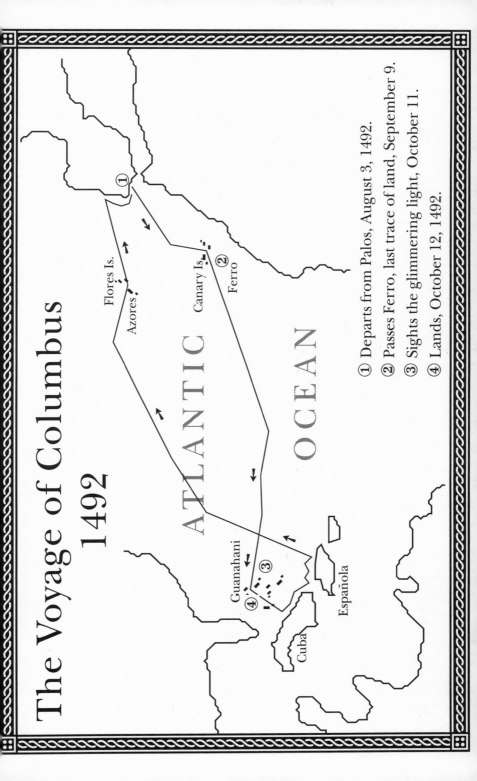

The Voyage of Columbus
1492

ATLANTIC

OCEAN

Flores Is.

Azores

Canary Is.

Ferro

① Departs from Palos, August 3, 1492.

② Passes Ferro, last trace of land, September 9.

③ Sights the glimmering light, October 11.

④ Lands, October 12, 1492.

Guanahani

① ② ③ ④

Española

Cuba

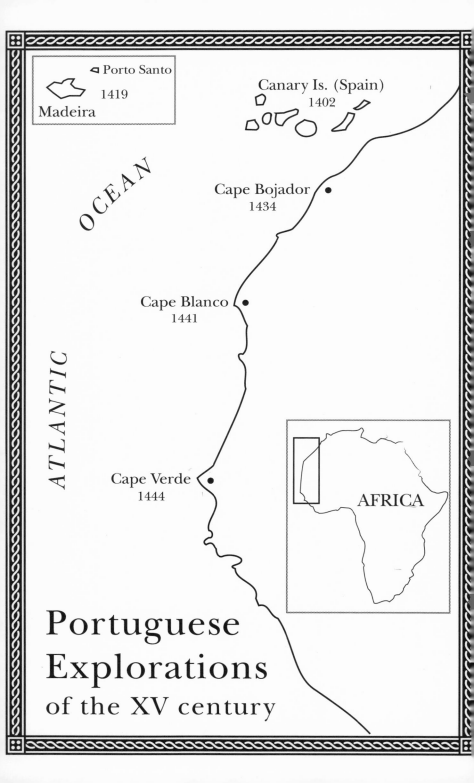

Porto Santo
Madeira 1419

Canary Is. (Spain)
1402

OCEAN

Cape Bojador
1434

ATLANTIC

Cape Blanco
1441

Cape Verde
1444

AFRICA

Portuguese
Explorations
of the XV century

1

t the beginning of the fifteenth century, when the most intelligent minds were seeking in every direction for the scattered lights of geographical knowledge, a profound ignorance prevailed among the learned as to the western regions of the Atlantic; its vast waters were regarded with awe and wonder, seeming to bound the world as with a chaos, into which conjecture could not penetrate, and enterprise feared to adventure. We need no greater proof of this, than the description given of the Atlantic by Xerif al Idrisi[1] surnamed the Nubian, an eminent Arabian writer, whose countrymen possessed all that was known of geography in the middle ages.

"The ocean," he observes, "encircles the ultimate bounds of the inhabited earth, and all beyond it is unknown. No one has been able to verify anything concerning it, on account of its difficult and perilous navigation, its great obscurity, its profound depth, and frequent tempests; through fear of its mighty fishes, and its haughty winds; yet there are many islands in it, some of which are peopled, and others uninhabited. There is no mariner who dares to enter into its deep waters; or if any have done so, they have merely kept along its coasts, fearful of departing from them. The waves of this ocean, although they roll as high as mountains, yet maintain themselves without breaking; for if they broke, it would be impossible for a ship to plough them."

It is the object of the following work to relate the deeds and fortunes of the mariner, who first had the judgment to divine, and the intrepidity to brave, the mysteries of this perilous deep; and who, by his hardy genius, his inflexible constancy, and his heroic courage, brought the ends of the earth into communication with each other. The narrative of his troubled life is the link which connects the history of the old world with that of the new.

2

BIRTH, PARENTAGE, EDUCATION, AND
EARLY LIFE OF COLUMBUS.

hristopher Columbus, or Colombo, as the name is written in Italian, was born in the city of Genoa, about the year 1435-6, of poor but reputable and meritorious parentage. He was the son of Domenico Colombo, a wool-comber, and Susanna Fontanarossa, his wife; and his ancestors seem to have followed the same trade for several generations in Genoa.

Columbus was the oldest of four children; having two brothers, Bartholomew and Giacomo, or, as his name is translated into Spanish, Diego, and one sister, of whom nothing is known, excepting that she was married to a person in obscure life, called Giacomo Bavarello.

While very young, Columbus was taught reading, writing, grammar, and arithmetic, and made some proficiency in drawing. He soon evinced a strong passion for geographical knowledge, and an irresistible inclination for the sea; and in after-life, when he looked back upon his career with a solemn and superstitious feeling, he regarded this early determination of his mind as an impulse from the Deity, guiding him to the studies, and inspiring him with the inclinations, proper to fit him for the high decrees he was destined to accomplish. His father, seeing the bent of his mind, endeavored to give him an education suitable for maritime life. He sent him, therefore, to the university of Pavia , where he was instructed in geometry, geography, astronomy, and navigation; he acquired also a familiar knowledge of the Latin tongue, which at that time was the medium of instruction, and the language of the schools. (Some authorities express doubts about his having attended the university.) He remained but a short time at Pavia, barely sufficient to give him the rudiments of the necessary sciences; the thorough acquaintance with them which he displayed in after-life, must have been the result of diligent self-schooling, and of casual hours of study, amidst the cares and vicissitudes of a rugged and wandering life.

Shortly after leaving the university, he entered into nautical life, and, according to his own account, began to navigate at fourteen years of age. A complete obscurity rest upon this part of his history. It is supposed he made his first voyages with one Colombo, a hardy captain of the seas, who had risen to some distinction by his bravery, and who was a distant connection of his family. This veteran is occasionally mentioned in old chronicles; sometimes as commanding a squadron of his own, sometimes as being an admiral in the Genoese service. He appears to have been bold and adventurous, ready to fight in any cause, and to seek quarrel wherever it might lawfully be found.

The seafaring life in those days was peculiarly full of hazard and enterprise. Even a commercial expedition resembled a warlike cruise, and the maritime merchant had often to fight his way from port to port.

Piracy was almost legalized. The frequent feuds between the Italian states; the cruisings of the Catalonians; the armadas fitted out by noblemen, who were petty sovereigns in their own domains; the roving ships and squadrons of private adventurers; and the holy wars waged with the Mohammedan powers, rendered the narrow seas, to which navigation was principally confined, scenes of the most hardy encounters and trying reverses. Such was the rugged school in which Columbus was reared, and such the rugged teacher that first broke him to naval discipline.

The first voyage in which we hear any account of his being engaged, was in a naval expedition fitted out at Genoa in 1459, by John of Anjou,[2] Duke of Calabria, to make a descent upon Naples, in the hope of recovering that kingdom for his father, King Reinier or Renato, otherwise called Renè, Count de Provence. In this enterprise the republic of Genoa aided with ships and money, and many private adventurers fitted out ships and galleys, and engaged under the banners of Anjou. Among the number was the hardy veteran Colombo, who had command of a squadron, and with him sailed his youthful relation.

There is an interval of several years, during which we have but one or two shadowy traces of Columbus, who is supposed to have been principally engaged in the Mediterranean, and up the Levant, sometimes in voyages of commerce, sometimes in warlike contests between the Italian states, sometimes in pious and predatory expeditions against the Infidels, during which time he was often under the perilous command of his old fighting relation, the veteran Colombo.

3

he career of modern discovery had commenced shortly before the time of Columbus, and, at the period of which we are treating, was prosecuted with great activity by Portugal. The
rediscovery of the Canary Islands, in the fourteenth century, and the occasional voyages made to them, and to
the opposite shores of Africa, had first turned the attention of mankind in that direction. The grand impulse to
discovery, however, was given by Prince Henry of Portugal,[3] son of John the First, surnamed the Avenger, and
Phillippa of Lancaster, sister of Henry the Fourth of
England. Having accompanied his father into Africa, in
the expedition against the Moors, Prince Henry received much information at Ceuta concerning the coast
of Guinea, and other regions entirely unknown to Europeans; and conceived an idea that important discoveries
were to be made, by navigating along the western coast
of Africa. On returning to Portugal, he pursued the

vein of inquiry thus accidentally opened. Abandoning the court, he returned to a country retreat in the Algarve, near to Sagres, in the neighborhood of Cape St. Vincent, and in full view of the ocean. Here he drew round him men eminent in science, and gave himself up to those branches of study connected with the maritime arts. He made himself master of all the geographical knowledge of the ancients, and of the astronomical science of the Arabians of Spain. The result of his studies was a firm conviction that Africa was circumnavigable, and that it was possible, by keeping along its shores, to arrive at India.

For a long time past, the opulent trade of Asia had been monopolized by the Italians; who had their commercial establishments at Constantinople, and in the Black Sea. Thither all the precious commodities of the East were conveyed by a circuitous and expensive internal route, to be thence distributed over Europe. The republics of Venice and Genoa had risen to power and opulence, in consequence of this monopoly; their merchants emulated the magnificence of princes, and held Europe, in a manner, tributary to their commerce. It was the grand idea of Prince Henry, by circumnavigating Africa, to open an easier and less expensive route to the source of this commerce, to turn it suddenly into a new and simple channel, and to pour it out in a golden tide upon his country. He was before the age in thought, and had to struggle hard against the ignorance and prejudices of mankind in the prosecution of his design. Navigation was yet in its infancy; mariners feared to venture far from the coast, or out of sight of its landmarks; and they looked with awe at the vast and unknown expanse of the Atlantic; they cherished the old belief that the earth at the equator was girdled by a torrid zone, separating the hemispheres by a region of impassable heat; and they had a superstitious belief, that whoever doubled Cape Bojador would never return.

Prince Henry called in the aid of science to dispel these errors. He established a naval college and observatory at Sagres, and invited thither the most eminent professors of the nautical faculties. The effects of this establishment were soon apparent. A vast improvement took place in maps and charts; the compass was brought into more general use; the Portuguese marine became signalized for its hardy enterprises; Cape Bojador was doubled; the region of the tropics penetrated and divested of its fancied terrors; the greater part of the African coast, from Cape Blanco to Cape de Verde, explored, and the Cape de Verde and Azore Islands discovered. To secure the full enjoyment of these territories, Henry obtained a papal bull, investing the crown of Portugal with sovereign authority over all the lands it might discover in the Atlantic, to India inclusive. Henry died on the 13th of November, 1473, before he had accomplished the great object of his ambition; but he had lived long enough to behold, through his means, his native country in a grand career of prosperity.

The news of the Portuguese discoveries drew the attention of the world, and the learned, the curious, and the adventurous, resorted to Lisbon to engage in the enterprises continually fitting out. Among the rest, Columbus arrived there about the year 1470. He was at that time in the full vigor of manhood, and of an engaging presence; and here it may not be improper to draw his portrait, according to the minute descriptions given of him by his contemporaries. He was tall, well-formed, and muscular, and of an elevated and dignified demeanor. His visage was long, and neither full nor meagre; his complexion fair and freckled, and inclined to ruddy; his nose aquiline, his cheek bones were rather high, his eyes light gray, and apt to enkindle; his whole countenance had an air of authority. His hair, in his youthful days, was of a light color, but care and trouble soon turned it gray, and at thirty years of age it was quite white.

Portrait

While at Lisbon, he was accustomed to attend religious service at the chapel of the Convent of All Saints. Here he became acquainted with a lady of rank, named Doña Felipa, who resided in the convent. She was the daughter of Bartolomeo Moñis de Palestrello, an Italian cavalier, lately deceased, who had been one of the most distinguished navigators under Prince Henry, and had colonized and governed the island of Porto Santo. The acquaintance soon ripened into attachment, and ended in marriage. It appears to have been a match of mere affection, as the lady had little or no fortune.

The newly-married couple resided with the mother of the bride. The latter, perceiving the interest which her son-in-law took in nautical affairs, used to relate to him all she knew of the voyages and expeditions of her late husband, and delivered to him all his charts, journals, and other manuscripts. By these means, Columbus became acquainted with the routes of the Portuguese, and their plans and ideas; and, having by his marriage and residence become naturalized in Portugal, he sailed occasionally in the expeditions to the coast of Guinea. When at home, he supported his family by making maps and charts; and though his means were scanty, he appropriated a part to the education of his younger brothers, and the succor of his aged father at Genoa.

From Lisbon he removed for a time to the recently discovered island of Porto Santo, where his wife had inherited some property, and during his residence there she bore him a son, whom he named Diego. His wife's sister was married to Pedro Correo, a navigator of note, who had at one time been governor of Porto Santo. In the familiar intercourse of domestic life, their conversation frequently turned upon the discoveries of the Atlantic islands, and the African coasts, upon the long-sought-for route to India, and upon the possibility of unknown lands existing in the west. It was a period of general excitement, with all who were connected with marine life, or who resided in the vicinity of the ocean. The recent discoveries had inflamed their imaginations and had filled them with ideas of other islands of greater wealth and beauty, yet to be discovered in the boundless wastes of the Atlantic.

The voyages Columbus had made to Guinea, and his frequent occupation in making maps and charts, had led him more and more to speculate on the great object of geographical enterprise; but while others were slowly and painfully seeking a route to India, by following up the coast of Africa, his daring genius conceived the bold idea of turning his prow directly to the west, and seeking the desired land by a route across the Atlantic. Having once conceived this idea, it is interesting to notice from what a mass of acknowledged facts, rational hypotheses, fanciful narrations, and popular rumors, his grand project of discovery was wrought out by the strong workings of his vigorous mind.

4

We have a record of the determination of Columbus to seek a western route to India, as early as the year 1474, in a correspondence which he held with Paulo Toscanelli,[4] a learned cosmographer of Florence. Toscanelli set it down as a fundamental principle, that the earth was a terraqueous globe, which might be traveled round from east to west, and that men stood foot to foot when on opposite points. A navigator, therefore, by pursuing a direct course from east to west, must arrive at the extremity of Asia, or discover any intervening land. Toscanelli encouraged Columbus in seeking India by a western course, assuring him that the distance could not be more than four thousand miles in a direct line from Lisbon to the province of Mangi, near Cathay, since ascertained to be the northern coast of China.[5]

The letter of Paulo Toscanelli was accompanied by a map, projected partly according to Ptolemy,[6] and partly according to the descriptions of Marco Polo,[7] a Vene-

tian traveler, who, in the fourteenth century, had penetrated the remote parts of Asia, far beyond the regions
laid down by Ptolemy. The eastern coast of Asia was de-
picted in front of the coasts of Africa and Europe, with
a moderate space of ocean between them, in which
were placed, at convenient distances, Cipango, Antilla [8]
and other islands. By this conjectural map Columbus
governed himself in his first voyage.

Besides these learned authorities, Columbus was at-
tentive to every gleam of information bearing upon his
theory, that might be derived from veteran mariners,
and the inhabitants of the lately discovered islands, who
were placed in a manner, on the frontier posts of geographical knowledge. One Antonio Leone, an inhabi-
tant of Madeira, told him that in sailing westward one
hundred leagues, he had seen three islands at a distance. A mariner of Port St. Mary, also, asserted, that in
the course of a voyage to Ireland, he had seen land to
the west, which the ship's company took for some extreme part of Tartary.[9] One Martin Vicenti, a pilot in
the service of the king of Portugal, assured Columbus
that, after sailing four hundred and fifty leagues to the
west of Cape St. Vincent, he had taken from the water a
piece of carved wood, evidently not labored with an
iron instrument. As the wind had drifted it from the
west, it might have come from some unknown land in
that direction.

Pedro Correo, brother-in-law of Columbus, also informed him, that he had seen a similar piece of wood, on the island of Porto Santo, which had drifted from the same quarter, and he had heard from the king of Portugal that reeds of an immense size had floated to those islands from the west, which Columbus supposed to be the kind of reeds of enormous magnitude described by Ptolemy as growing in India. Trunks of huge pine trees, of a kind that did not grow upon any of the islands, had been wafted to the Azores by westerly winds. The inhabitants also informed him that the bodies of two dead men had been cast upon the island of Flores, whose features had caused great wonder and speculation, being different from those of any known race of people.

Such are the principal grounds on which, according to Fernando Columbus, his father proceeded from one position to another of his theory. It is evident, however, that the grand argument which induced him to his enterprise, was the one first cited; namely, that the most eastern part of Asia known to the ancients could not be separated from the Azores by more that a third of the circumference of the globe; that the intervening space must, in a great measure, be filled up by the unknown residue of Asia; and that, as the circumference of the world was less than was generally supposed, the Asiatic shores could easily be attained by a moderate voyage to the west. It is singular how much the success of this great enterprise depended upon two happy errors, the imaginary extent of Asia to the east, and the supposed smallness of the earth; both errors of the most learned and profound philosophers, but without which Columbus would hardly have ventured into the western regions of the Atlantic, in whose unknown and perhaps immeasurable waste of waters, he might perish before he could reach a shore.

5

t this juncture, John the Second[10] ascended the throne of Portugal. He had imbibed the passion for discovery from his grand-uncle, Prince Henry, and with his reign all its activity revived.

Impatient of the tardiness with which his discoveries advanced along the coast of Africa, and eager to realize the splendid project of Prince Henry, and conduct the Portuguese flag into the Indian seas, John the Second called upon his men of science, to devise some means of giving greater scope and certainty to navigation. His two physicians, Roderigo and Joseph, the latter a Jew, who were the most able astronomers and cosmographers of his kingdom, together with the celebrated Martin Behaim[11] entered into a consultation on the subject; and the result of their conferences was, the application of the astrolabe to navigation, an instrument to measure the height of the sun or stars above the horizon. This invention was one of those timely occurrences which seemed to have something providential in them. It was the one thing wanting to facilitate an intercourse across the deep, and to cast navigation loose from its long bondage to the land. Science had thus prepared guides for discovery across the trackless ocean, and had divested the enterprise of Columbus of that extremely hazardous character, which had been so great an obstacle to its accomplishment. It was immediately after this event that he solicited an audience of the king of Portugal, to lay before him his great project of discovery. This is the first proposition of which we have any clear and indisputable record.

Columbus obtained a ready audience of King John, who was extremely liberal in encouraging and rewarding nautical enterprise. He explained to the monarch his theory, and proposed, in case the king would furnish him with ships and men, to conduct them by a shorter route to the richest countries of the East, to touch at the opulent island of Cipango, and to establish a communication with the territories of the Grand Khan, the most splendid, powerful, and wealthy of oriental potentates.

King John listened attentively to the proposition of Columbus, and referred it to a learned junta composed of Masters Roderigo and Joseph, and the king's confessor, Diego Ortiz, bishop of Ceuta, a man greatly reputed for his learning, a Castilian by birth, and generally called Cazadilla, from the name of his birthplace. This scientific body treated the project as extravagant and visionary. Still the king was not satisfied, but convoked his council, composed of persons of the greatest learning in the kingdom, and asked their advice. In this assembly Cazadilla, the bishop of Ceuta, opposed the theory of Columbus, as destitute of reason, and indeed evinced a cold and narrow spirit, hostile to all discovery. The decision of the council was equally unfavorable with that of the junta, and the proposition of Columbus was rejected.

Certain of the counsellors, and particularly the bishop of Cazadilla, seeing that the king was dissatisfied with their decision and retained a lurking inclination for the enterprise, suggested a stratagem by which all its advantages might be secured, without committing the dignity of the crown by entering into formal negotiations about a scheme, which might prove a mere chimera. The king, in an evil hour, departed from his usual justice and generosity, and had the weakness to permit the stratagem. These crafty counsellors then procured from Columbus, as if to assist them in their deliberations, a detailed plan of his proposed voyage, with the charts by which he intended to shape his course. While they held him in suspense, awaiting their decision, they privately dispatched a caravel to pursue the designated route.

The caravel took its departure from the Cape de Verde Islands, and stood westward for several days. The weather grew stormy, and the pilots having no zeal to stimulate them, and seeing nothing but an immeasurable waste of wild tumbling waves, still extending before them, lost all courage, and put back to the Cape de Verde Islands, and thence to Lisbon, excusing their own want of resolution, by ridiculing the project as extravagant and irrational.

This unworthy attempt to defraud him of his enterprise roused the indignation of Columbus, and, though King John, it is said, showed a disposition to renew the negotiation, he resolutely declined. His wife had been for some time dead, the domestic tie which had bound him to Portugal, therefore, being broken, he determined to abandon a country where he had been treated with so little faith. Like most projectors, while engaged in schemes which held out promise of incalculable wealth, he had suffered his affairs to run to ruin, and was in danger of being arrested for debt. This has been given as the reason for his leaving Portugal in a secret manner, which he did towards the end of 1484, taking with him his son Diego, as yet a mere child.

An interval now occurs of about a year, during which the movements of Columbus are involved in uncertainty. It has been asserted by a modern Spanish historian of merit, that he departed immediately for Genoa, where he repeated in person the proposition which he had formerly made to the government by letter. The republic of Genoa, however, was languishing under a long decline, and was embarrassed by ruinous wars. Thus, Genoa, disheartened by reverses, rejected a proposition which would have elevated the republic to tenfold splendor, and might for a long time have perpetuated the golden wand of commerce in the failing grasp of Italy.

From Genoa, it has been said, but equally without positive proof, that Columbus carried his proposal to Venice, but that it was declined in consequence of the critical state of national affairs. Different authors agree, that about this time he visited his aged father, and made such arrangements for his comfort as his own poor means afforded, and that having thus performed the duties of a pious son, he departed once more to try his fortunes in foreign courts. About this time, also, he engaged his brother Bartholomew to sail for England, to lay his propositions before Henry the Seventh, whom he had heard extolled for his wisdom and munificence. For himself, he sailed for Spain, where he appears to have arrived in great poverty, for this course of fruitless solicitation had exhausted all his means; nor is it one of the least extraordinary circumstances in his eventful life, that he had, in a manner, to beg his way from court to court, to offer to princes the discovery of a world.

6

he first trace we have of Columbus in Spain, is gathered from the manuscript documents of the celebrated lawsuit, which took place a few years after his death, between his son Don Diego and the crown. It is contained in the deposition of one Garcia Fernandez, a physician, resident in the little sea-port of Palos de Moguer, in Andalusia. About half a league from Palos, on a solitary height overlooking the seacoast, and surrounded by a forest of pine trees, there stood, and stands at the present day, an ancient convent of Franciscan friars, dedicated to Santa Maria de La Rabida. A stranger traveling on foot, accompanied by a young boy, stopped one day at the gate of the convent, and asked of the porter a little bread and water for his child. While receiving this humble refreshment, the guardian of the convent, Friar Juan Perez de Marchena, happening to pass by, was struck with the appearance of the stranger, and, observing from his air and accent that he was a foreigner, entered into conversation with him. That stranger was Columbus, accompanied by his young son Diego. He was on his way to the neighboring town of Huelva, to seek a brother-in-law, who had married a sister of his deceased wife.

The guardian was an intelligent man, and accquainted with geographical and nautical science. He was interested by the conversation of Columbus, and struck with the grandeur of his plans. He detained him as his guest, and being diffident of his own judgment, sent for a scientific friend to converse with him. That friend was Garcia Fernandez, the physician of Palos, the same who furnishes this interesting testimony, and who became equally convinced with the friar of the correctness of the theory of Columbus. Several veteran pilots and mariners of Palos, also were consulted during the conferences at the convent, who stated various facts observed in the course of their experience, which seemed to corroborate the idea of western lands in the Atlantic. But the conviction of the friar was still more confirmed, by the hearty concurrence of an important personage in that maritime neighborhood, one Martin Alonzo Pinzon, resident of the town of Palos, one of the most intelligent sea captains of the day, and the head of a family of wealthy and distinguished navigators. Pinzon not only gave the project of Columbus his decided approbation, but offered to engage in it with purse and person.

Fray Juan Perez, being now fully persuaded of the importance of the proposed enterprise, advised Columbus to repair to court, and make his propositions to the Spanish sovereigns, offering to give him a letter of recommendation to his friend, Fernando de Talavera, prior of the convent of Prado, and confessor to the queen, and a man of great political influence, through whose means he would, no doubt, immediately obtain royal audience and favor. Martin Alonzo Pinzon, also, generously offered to furnish him with money for the journey, and the friar took charge of his youthful son, Diego, to maintain and educate him in the convent. Thus aided and encouraged, and elated with fresh hopes, Columbus took leave of the little junta at La Rabida, and set out, in the spring of 1486, for the Castilian court which had just assembled at Cordova, where the sovereigns were fully occupied with their chivalrous enterprise for the conquest of Granada. And here it is proper to give a brief description of these princes, who performed such an important part in the events of this history.

It has been well observed of Ferdinand and Isabella,[12] that they lived together, not like man and wife, whose estates are in common, under the orders of the husband, but like two monarchs, strictly allied. They had separate claims to sovereignty, in virtue of their separate kingdoms, and held separate councils. Yet they were so

happily united by common interests, and a great deference for each other, that this double administration
never prevented a unity of purpose and action. All acts
of sovereignty were executed in both their names; all
public writings subscribed with both their signatures;
their likenesses were stamped together on the public
coin; and the royal seal displayed the united arms of
Castile and Aragon.

Ferdinand possessed a clear and comprehensive genius, and great penetration. He was equable in temper,
indefatigable in business, a great observer of men, and
is extolled by Spanish writers as unparalleled in the science of the cabinet. It has been maintained by writers
of other nations, however, and apparently with reason,
that he was bigoted in religion, and craving rather than
magnanimous in his ambition; that he made war less
like a paladin than a prince, less for glory than for mere
dominion, and that his policy was cold, selfish, and art-
ful. He was called the wise and prudent in Spain; in Italy, the pious; in France and England, the ambitious and
perfidious.

Contemporary writers have been enthusiastic in their
descriptions of Isabella, but time has sanctioned their
eulogies. She was of middle size, and well formed; with
a fair complexion, auburn hair, and clear blue eyes.
There was a mingled gravity and sweetness in her countenance, and a singular modesty, gracing, as it did,

great firmness of purpose and earnestness of spirit. Though strongly attached to her husband, and studious of his fame, yet she always maintained her distinct rights as an allied prince. She exceeded him in beauty, personal dignity, acuteness of genius, and grandeur of soul. Combining the active and resolute qualities of man, with the softer charities of woman, she mingled in the warlike councils of her husband, and being inspired with a truer idea of glory, infused a more lofty and generous temper into his subtle and calculating policy.

It is in the civil history of their reign, however, that the character of Isabella shines most illustrious. Her fostering and maternal care was continually directed to reform the laws, and heal the ills engendered by a long course of civil wars. She assembled round her the ablest men in literature and science, and directed herself by their counsels in encouraging literature and the arts. She promoted the distribution of honors and rewards for the promulgation of knowledge, fostered the recently invented art of printing, and through her patronage Salamanca rose to that eminence which it assumed among the learned institutions of the age. Such was the noble woman who was destined to acquire immortal renown by her spirited patronage of the discovery of the new world.

7

PROPOSITIONS OF COLUMBUS TO
THE COURT OF CASTILE.

hen Columbus arrived at Cordova, he found it in all the bustle of military preparation. The two rival Moorish kings of Granada had formed a coalition, and the Castilian sovereigns had summoned all their chivalry to assemble for a grand campaign. Every day witnessed the arrival of some Spanish noble, with a splendid retinue, and a brilliant array of household troops. The court was like a military camp; every avenue was crowded by warlike grandees and hardy cavaliers, who had distinguished themselves in this Moorish war. This was an unpropitious moment for an application like that of Columbus. Everybody was engrossed by the opening campaign. Even Fernando de Talavera, who was to have been his great patron and protector, and his organ of communication with the sovereigns, was completely taken up with military concerns, being one of the clerical advisers, who surrounded the queen in this, as it was termed, holy war. The letter of recommendation from the worthy Fray Juan

Perez, which was to have secured the powerful influence of Talavera, seems to have had but little effect upon the prior, who listened coldly to Columbus, and looked upon his plan as extravagant and impossible.

So far, therefore, from receiving immediate patronage from the sovereigns, Columbus found it impossible to obtain even a hearing. It is a question even, whether, for some time, his application reached their ears. If Fernando de Talavera did mention it to them, it must have been in disparaging terms, such as rather to destroy than excite interest in its favor. The campaign opened almost immediately; the king took the field in person; the queen was fully occupied by the hurrying concerns of the war, and was part of the time present in the camp; it would have been in vain, therefore, at such a moment, to expect attention to a scheme of foreign discovery, founded on principles which required calm and learned investigation.

During the summer and autumn of 1486, Columbus remained at Cordova, waiting for a more favorable opportunity to urge his suit, and trusting to time and assiduity to gain him converts among the intelligent and powerful. He was in indigent circumstances, and earned a scanty support by making maps and charts. Some scoffed at him as a mere dreamer, others stigmatized him as an adventurer; the very children, it is said, pointed to their foreheads as he passed, being taught to consider him a kind of madman.

While thus lingering in Cordova, he became attached to Doña Beatrix Enriquez, a lady of that city, of a noble family. Like most of the circumstances of this part of his life, his connection with this lady is wrapped in obscurity, but appears never to have been sanctioned by marriage. She was the mother of his second son Fernando, who became his historian, and whom he always treated on terms of perfect equality with his legitimate son Diego.

By degrees the theory of Columbus began to obtain proselytes. Alonzo de Quintanilla, comptroller of the finances of Castile, became a warm advocate of his theory, and received him as a guest into his house. He was countenanced also by Antonio Geraldini, the pope's nuncio, and his brother, Alexander Geraldini, preceptor to the younger children of Ferdinand and Isabella. By these friends he was introduced to the celebrated Pedro Gonzalez de Mendoza,[13] archbishop of Toledo, and grand cardinal of Spain. This was the most important personage about the court, he was always with the king and queen, who never took any measure of consequence without consulting him, and was facetiously called the third king of Spain. He was an elegant scholar, a man of sound understanding, and of great quickness and capacity in business. The clear-headed cardinal was pleased with the noble and earnest, manner of Columbus; he listened to him with profound attention, felt the importance of his project and the force of his arguments, and became at once a firm and serviceable friend. Through his intercession the royal audience was at length obtained.

Columbus appeared in the presence of the king with modesty, yet self-possession, inspired by a consciousness of the dignity and importance of his errand. Ferdinand was too keen a judge of men not to appreciate the character of Columbus. He perceived, also, that his scheme had scientific and practical foundation; and his ambition was excited by the possibility of discoveries far exceeding in importance those which had shed such glory upon Portugal. Still, as usual, he was cool and wary. He ordered Fernando de Talavera, the prior of Prado, to assemble the most learned astronomers and cosmographers of the kingdom, to hold a conference with Columbus. They were to examine him upon the grounds of his theory, and afterwards to consult together, and report their opinion as to its merits. Columbus now considered the day of success at hand. From the dispassionate examination of such a body of sages, he could not but anticipate the triumphant verdict.

8

he interesting conference took place at Salamanca, the great seat of learning in Spain. It was held in the Dominican convent of St. Stephen, the most scientific college in the university, in which Columbus was lodged and entertained with great hospitality during the course of the examination. The board of conference was composed of professors of the university, together with various dignitaries of the church, and learned friars. No tribunal could bear a front of more imposing wisdom; yet Columbus soon discovered that ignorance and illiberality may sometimes lurk under the very robes of science.

The hall of the old convent presented a striking spectacle. A simple mariner standing forth in the midst of an imposing array of clerical and collegiate sages; maintaining his theory with natural eloquence, and, as it were, pleading the cause of the new world. We are told, that when he began to state the grounds of his theory, the friars of St. Stephen alone paid attention to him. The others appeared to have intrenched themselves behind one dogged position, namely, that, after so many profound philosophers had occupied themselves in geographical investigations, and so many able navigators had been voyaging about the world for ages, it was a great presumption in an ordinary man to suppose that there remained such a vast discovery for him to make.

Thus, at the very threshold of the discussion, Columbus was assailed with citations from the Bible, The possibility of the existence of antipodes in the southern hemisphere, though maintained by the wisest of the ancients, was disputed by some of the sages of Salamanca, on the authority of Lactantius [14] and St. Augustine,[15] those two great luminaries of what has been called the golden age of ecclesiastical learning. ("Is there any one so foolish," asks Lactantius, "as to believe that there are antipodes with their feet opposite to ours; people who walk with their heels upward and their heads hanging down? That there is a part of the world in which all things are topsy-turvy; where the trees grow with their branches downward, and where it rains, hails, and snows upwards?" The idea of the roundness of the earth, he adds, "was the cause of inventing this fable; for these philosophers, having once erred, go on in their absurdities, defending one with another."

Objections of a graver nature, and more dignified tone, were advanced on the authority of St. Augustine. He pronounces the doctrine of antipodes incompatible with the historical foundations of our faith; since, to assert that there were inhabited lands on the opposite side of the globe, would be to maintain that there were nations not descended from Adam, it being impossible for them to have passed the intervening ocean. This would be, therefore, to discredit the Bible, which expressly declares, that all men are descended from one common parent. As for steering to the west in search of India, they observed that the circumference of the earth must be so great as to require at least three years to the voyage, and those who should undertake it must perish of hunger and thirst, from the impossibility of carrying provisions for so long a period. Not the least absurd objection advanced, was, that should a ship even succeed in reaching the extremity of India, she could never get back again, for the rotundity of the globe would present a kind of mountain, up which it would be impossible for her to sail with the most favorable wind.

It is but justice to add, that many of his learned hearers were convinced by his reasoning, and warmed by his eloquence; among the number of these was Diego de Deza, a worthy friar of the order of St. Dominic, at that time professor of theology in the convent of St. Stephen, but who became afterwards archbishop of Seville, the second ecclesiastical dignity of Spain. He was an able and erudite man, above the narrow bigotry of bookish lore, and could appreciate the value of wisdom, even when uttered by unlearned lips. He seconded Columbus with all his powers and influence, and by their united efforts, they brought over several of the most intelligent men of the assembly.

After this celebrated examination of Columbus, the board held occasional conferences, but without coming to any decision; Fernando de Talavera, to whom the matter was especially intrusted, had too little esteem for it, and was too much occupied by the stir and bustle of public concerns, to press it to a conclusion; his departure with the court from Cordova, early in the spring of 1487, put an end to the consultations, and left Columbus in a state of the most tantalizing suspense.

For several years he followed the movements of the court, continually flattered with hopes of success. Conferences were appointed at various places, but the tempest of warlike affairs, which hurried the court from place to place, and gave it the bustle and confusion of a camp, continually swept away all matters of less immediate importance. He was present at the sieges and surrenders of Malaga and Baza and beheld El Zagal,[16] the elder of the two rival kings of Granada, yield up his crown and possessions to the Spanish sovereigns. During the siege of Baza, two reverend friars, guardians of the holy sepulchre at Jerusalem, arrived in the Spanish camp, bearing a menace from the Grand Sultan of Egypt,[17] that he would put to death all the Christians in his dominions, and destroy the sepulchre, if the sovereigns did not desist from the war against the Moslems of Granada. It is probable that the pious indignation excited by this threat in the bosom of Columbus, gave the first rise to a resolution which he entertained to the day of his death; this was, to devote the profits which he anticipated from his discoveries, to a crusade for the rescue of the holy sepulchre.

During this long course of application, Columbus partly defrayed his expenses by making maps and charts. He was occasionally assisted, also, by the purse of the worthy Friar Diego de Deza, and was sometimes a guest of Alonzo de Quintanilla. It is due to the sovereigns to say, also, that he was attached to the royal suite, and sums issued to defray his expenses, and lodgings provided for him, when summoned to follow this rambling and warlike court. Whenever the sovereigns had an interval of leisure, there seems to have been a disposition to attend to his proposition; but the hurry and tempest of the war returned, and the question was again swept away.

At length, in the winter of 1491, when the sovereigns were preparing to depart on their final campaign in the vega or fertile plain of Granada, Columbus, losing all patience, pressed for a decisive reply, and Fernando de Talavera was ordered, 'therefore, to hold a final conference, and to report the decision of his learned brethren. He obeyed, and informed their majesties that the majority of the junta condemned the scheme as vain and impossible, and considered it unbecoming such great princes to engage in an undertaking of the kind, on such weak grounds as had been advanced.

A degree of consideration, however, had gradually grown up at court for the enterprise, and notwithstanding this unfavorable report, the sovereigns were unwilling to close the door on a project which might be of such important advantages. They informed Columbus, therefore, that the great cares and expenses of the war rendered it impossible for them to engage in any new enterprises for the present; but that, when the war should be concluded, they would have leisure and inclination to treat with him concerning his propositions.

This was but a starved reply to receive after so many years of weary attendance; Columbus considered it a mere evasion of the sovereigns to relieve themselves from his importunity, and, giving up all hope of countenance from the throne, he turned his back upon Seville, filled with disappointment and indignation.

9

 olumbus now looked round in search of
some other source of patronage. He had received favorable letters both from the kings
of England and of France; the king of Portugal, also,
had invited him to return to his court; but he appears
to have become attached to Spain, probably from its being the residence of Beatrix Enriquez, and his children.
He sought, therefore, to engage the patronage of some
one of those powerful Spanish grandees, who had vast
possessions, exercised feudal rights, and were petty sovereigns in their domains. Among these, were the dukes
of Medina Sidonia, and Medina Celi; both had princi-
palities lying along the seaboard, with armies of vassals,
and ports and shipping at their command. Columbus
had many interviews with the duke of Medina Sidonia,
who was tempted for a time by the splendid prospects
held out; but their very splendor threw a coloring of ex-
aggeration over the enterprise, and he finally rejected it
as the dream of an Italian visionary.

The duke of Medina Celi was still more favorable, and was actually on the point of granting him three or four caravels which lay ready for sea, in his harbor of Port St. Mary; but he suddenly changed his mind, fearing to awaken the jealousy of the crown, and to be considered as interfering with the views of the sovereigns, who he knew had been treating with Columbus. He advised him, therefore, to return once more to court, and he wrote a letter to the queen in favor of his project.

Columbus felt averse to the idea of subjecting himself again to the tantalizing delays and disappointments of the court, and determined to repair to Paris. He departed, therefore, for the convent of La Rabida, to seek his oldest son Diego, and leave him with his other son at Cordova.

When the worthy Friar Juan Perez de Marchena beheld Columbus arrive once more at the gate of his convent, after nearly seven years of fruitless solicitation at the court, and saw, by the humility of his garb, the poverty he had experienced, he was greatly moved; but when he found that he was on the point of leaving Spain, and carrying his proposition to another country, his patriotism took the alarm. He had been confessor to the queen, and knew her to be always accessible to persons of his sacred calling. He wrote a letter to her, therefore, earnestly vindicating the proposed scheme, and conjuring her not to turn a deaf ear to a matter of such vast importance; and he prevailed upon Columbus to delay his journey until an answer should be received.

The ambassador chosen by the little junta of the convent was one Sebastian Rodriguez, a pilot of Lepe, who acquitted himself faithfully, expeditiously, and successfully, in his embassy. He found access to the benignant princess in the royal camp at Santa Fé, before Granada, and delivered the epistle of the friar. He returned in fourteen days, with a letter from the queen, thanking Juan Perez for his timely services, and requesting him to repair immediately to the court, leaving Columbus in confident hope of hearing further from her. This royal epistle caused great exultation in the convent. No sooner did the warmhearted friar receive it, than he procured a mule, and departed instantly, before midnight, for the court.

His sacred office, and his former relation as father confessor, gave him immediate admission to the queen, and great freedom of counsel. It is probable Isabella had never heard the proposition of Columbus urged with such honest zeal and impressive eloquence. She was naturally more sanguine and susceptible than the king, and more open to warm and generous impulses. Moved by the representations of Juan Perez, she requested that Columbus might be again sent to her, and kindly bethinking herself of his poverty, and his humble plight, ordered that a sufficient sum of money should be forwarded to him to defray his traveling expenses, to provide him with a mule for his journey, and to furnish him with decent raiment, that he might make a respectable appearance at the court. Columbus lost no time in complying with the commands of the queen. He exchanged his threadbare garment for one of more courtly texture, and, purchasing a mule, set out once more, reanimated by fresh hopes, for the camp before Granada.

He arrived in time to witness the memorable surrender of that capital to the Spanish arms. He beheld Boabdil el Chico,[18] the last of the Moorish kings, sally forth from the Alhambra, and yield up the keys of that favorite seat of Moslem power; while the king and queen, with all the chivalry and magnificence of Spain, moved forward in proud and solemn procession, to receive this token of submission. It was one of the most brilliant triumphs in Spanish history. The air resounded with shouts of joy, with songs of triumph and hymns of thanksgiving. On every side were beheld military rejoicings and religious oblations. The court was thronged by the most illustrious of that warlike country, and stirring era; by the flower of its nobility, the most dignified of its prelacy, by bards and minstrels, and all the retinue of a romantic and picturesque age.

During this brilliant and triumphant scene, says an elegant Spanish writer, "A man, obscure and but little known, followed the court. Confounded in the crowd of importunate applicants, and feeding his imagination, in the corners of antechambers, with the pompous project of discovering a world, he was melancholy and beheld with indifference, almost with contempt, the conclusion of a conquest which swelled all bosoms with jubilee, and seemed to have reached the utmost bounds of desire. That man was Christopher Columbus."

The moment had now arrived, however, when the monarchs stood pledged to attend to his proposals. They kept their word, and persons of confidence were appointed to negotiate with him, among whom was Fernando de Talavera, who, by the recent conquest, had risen to be archbishop of Granada. At the very outset of their negotiation, however, unexpected difficulties arose. The principal stipulation of Columbus was, that he should be invested with the titles and privileges of admiral and viceroy, over the countries he should discover, with one tenth of all gains, either by trade or conquest. The courtiers who treated with him, were indignant at such a demand from one whom they had considered a needy adventurer.

One observed with a sneer, that it was a shrewd arrangement which he proposed, whereby he was certain of the profits and honors of a command, and had nothing to lose in case of failure. To this Columbus promptly replied, by offering to furnish one eighth of the cost, on condition of enjoying an eighth of the profits. His terms, however, were pronounced inadmissible, and others were offered, of more moderate nature, but he refused to cede one point of his demands, and the negotiation was broken off.

Indignant at the repeated disappointments he had experienced in Spain, he now determined to abandon it forever, and mounting his mule, sallied forth from Santa Fé (the camp town on the Jenil, near Granada, occupied by Ferdinand and Isabella) on his way to Cordova, with the intention of immediately proceeding from thence to France.

When the few friends, who were zealous believers in the theory of Columbus, saw him on the point of abandoning the country, they were filled with distress. Among the number was Luis de St. Angel, receiver of the ecclesiastical revenues of Aragon, and Alonzo de Quintanilla, who determined to make one bold effort to avert the evil. They hastened to the queen, and St. Angel addressed her with a courage and eloquence inspired by the exigency of the moment. He did not confine himself to entreaties, but almost mingled reproaches. He expressed his astonishment that a queen who had evinced the spirit to undertake so many great and perilous enterprises, should hesitate at one where the loss could be but trifling, while the gain might be incalculable; for all that was required for this great expedition was but two vessels, and about thirty thousand crowns, and Columbus himself had offered to bear an eighth of the expense. He reminded her how much might be done for the glory of God, the promotion of the Christian faith, and the extension of her own power and dominion, should this enterprise be adopted; but what cause of regret it would be to himself, of sorrow to her friends, and triumph to her enemies, should it be rejected by her, and accomplished by some other power. He vindicated the judgment of Columbus, and the soundness and practicability of his plans, and observed, that even a failure would reflect no disgrace upon the crown. It was worth the trouble and expense to clear up even a doubt, upon a matter of such importance, for it belonged to enlightened and magnanimous princes, to investigate questions of the kind, and to explore the wonders and secrets of the universe.

These, and many more arguments, were urged, with that persuasive power which honest zeal imparts. The generous spirit of Isabella was enkindled, and it seemed as if the subject, for the first time, broke upon her mind in its real grandeur. She declared her resolution to undertake the enterprise, but paused for a moment, remembering that King Ferdinand looked coldly on the affair, and that the royal treasury was absolutely drained by the war. Her suspense was but momentary. With an enthusiasm worthy of herself and of the cause, she exclaimed, "I undertake the enterprise for my own crown of Castile, and will pledge my jewels to raise the necessary funds." This was the proudest moment in the life of Isabella; it stamped her renown forever as the patroness of the discovery of the New World.

St. Angel, eager to secure this favorable resolution, assured her majesty that there would be no need of pledging her jewels, as he was ready to advance the necessary funds, as a loan, from the treasury of Aragon; his offer was gladly accepted.

Columbus had proceeded on his solitary journey across the vega of Granada, and had reached the bridge of Pinos, about two leagues from that city, a pass famous for bloody encounters during the Moorish wars. Here he was overtaken by a courier sent after him in all speed by the queen, requesting him to return to Santa Fé. He hesitated, for a moment, to subject himself again to the delays and equivocations of the court; but when he was informed that Isabella had positively undertaken the enterprise, and pledged her royal word, every doubt was dispelled, he turned the reins of his mule, and hastened back joyfully to Santa Fé, confiding implicitly in the noble probity of that princess.

10

n arriving at Santa Fé, Columbus had an immediate audience of the queen, and the benignity with which she received him, atoned for all past neglect. Through deference to the zeal she thus suddenly displayed, the king yielded his tardy concurrence, but Isabella was the soul of this grand enterprise. She was prompted by lofty and generous enthusiasm, while the king remained cold and calculating, in this as in all his other undertakings.

A perfect understanding being thus effected with the sovereigns, articles of agreement were drawn out by Juan de Coloma, the royal secretary. They were to the following effect:—

1. That Columbus should have, for himself, during his life, and his heirs and successors forever, the office of high admiral in all the seas, lands and continents, he

might discover, with similar honors and prerogatives to those enjoyed by the high admiral of Castile in his district.

2. That he should be viceroy and governor-general over all the said lands and continents, with the privilege of nominating three candidates for the government of each island or province, one of whom should be selected by the sovereigns.

3. That he should be entitled to one-tenth of all free profits, arising from the merchandise and productions of the countries within his admiralty.

4. That he, or his lieutenant, should be the sole judge of causes and disputes arising out of traffic between those countries and Spain.

5. That he might then, and at all aftertimes, contribute an eighth part of the expense of expeditions to sail to the countries he expected to discover, and should receive in consequence an eighth part of the profits.

These capitulations were signed by Ferdinand and Isabella, at the city of Santa Fé, in the vega or plain of Granada, on the 17th of April, 1492. All the royal documents, issued in consequence, bore equally the signatures of Ferdinand and Isabella.

One of the great objects held out by Columbus in his undertaking, was, the propagation of the Christian faith. He expected to arrive at the extremity of Asia, or

India, as it was then generally termed, at the vast empire of the Grand Khan.[19] Various missions had been sent, in former times, by popes and pious sovereigns, to instruct this oriental potentate, and his subjects, in the doctrines of Christianity. Columbus hoped to effect this grand work, and to spread the light of the true faith among the barbarous countries and nations that were to be discovered in the unknown parts of the East. Isabella, from pious zeal, and Ferdinand from mingled notions of bigotry and ambition, accorded with his views, and when he afterwards departed on this voyage, letters were actually given him, by the sovereigns, for the Grand Khan of Tartary.

The ardent enthusiasm of Columbus did not stop here. Recollecting the insolent threat once made by the sultan of Egypt, to destroy the holy sepulchre at Jerusalem, he proposed that the profits which might arise from his discoveries, should be consecrated to a crusade for the rescue of the holy edifice from the power of the Infidels. The sovereigns smiled at this sally of the imagination, and expressed themselves well pleased with the idea; but what they may have considered a mere momentary thought, was a deep and cherished design of Columbus.

The port of Palos de Moguer, in Andalusia, was fixed upon as the place where the armament for the expedition was to be fitted out, the community of the place being obliged, in consequence of some misdemeanor, to serve the crown for one year with two armed caravels. A royal order was issued, commanding the authorities of Palos to have these caravels ready for sea within ten days, and to yield them and their crews to the command of Columbus. The latter was likewise empowered to fit out a third vessel; nor was any restriction put upon his voyage, excepting that he should not go to the coast of Guinea, or any other of the lately discovered possessions of Portugal. Orders were likewise issued by the sovereigns, commanding the inhabitants of the seaboard of Andalusia, to furnish supplies and assistance of all kinds for the expedition, at a reasonable rate, and threatening severe penalties to such as should cause any impediment.

As a mark of particular favor to Columbus, Isabella, before his departure from the court, appointed his son Diego page to Prince Juan, the heir apparent, an honor granted only to the sons of persons of distinguished rank. Thus gratified in his dearest wishes, Columbus took leave of the court on the 12th of May, and set out joyfully for Palos.

When Columbus arrived at Palos, and presented himself once more before the gates of the convent of La Rabida, he was received with open arms by the worthy Juan Perez, and again entertained as his guest. The zealous friar accompanied him to the parochial church of

St. George, in Palos, where Columbus caused the royal order for the caravels to be read by a notary public, in presence of the authorities of the place. Nothing could equal the astonishment and horror of the people of this maritime community, when they heard of the nature of the expedition, in which they were ordered to engage. They considered the ships and crews demanded of them, in the light of sacrifices devoted to destruction. All the frightful tales and fables with which ignorance and superstition are prone to people obscure and distant regions, were conjured up concerning the unknown parts of the deep, and the boldest seamen shrunk from such a wild and chimerical cruise into the wilderness of the ocean.

Repeated mandates were issued by the sovereigns, ordering the magistrates of Palos, and the neighboring town of Moguer, to press into the service any Spanish vessels and crews they might think proper and threatening severe punishments on all who should prove refractory. It was all in vain, the communities of those places were thrown into complete confusion, tumults and altercations took place, but nothing of consequence was effected.

At length, Martin Alonzo Pinzon, the wealthy and enterprising navigator, who has already been mentioned, came forward and engaged personally in the expedition. He and his brother Vicente Yañez Pinzon, who was likewise a navigator of great courage and ability, possessed vessels, and had seamen in their employ. They were related to many of the seafaring inhabitants of Palos and Moguer, and had great influence throughout the neighborhood. It is supposed that they furnished Columbus with funds to pay the eighth share of the expense, which he had engaged to advance. They furnished two of the vessels required, and determined to sail in the expedition. Their example and persuasions had a wonderful effect; a great many of their relations and friends agreed to embark, and the vessels were ready for sea within a month after they had engaged in their enterprise.

During the equipment of the armament, various difficulties occurred. A third vessel, called the Pinta, had been pressed into the service, with its crew. The owners, Gomez Rascon, and Christoval Quintero, were strongly repugnant to the voyage, as were most of the mariners under them. These people, and their friends, endeavored in various ways to retard or defeat the voyage. The caulkers did their work in a careless manner, and, on being ordered to do it over again, absconded; several of the seamen who had enlisted willingly, repented and deserted. Everything had to be effected by harsh and arbitrary measures, and in defiance of popular opposition.

At length, by the beginning of August, every difficulty was vanquished, and the vessels were ready for sea. After all the objections made by various courts, to undertake this expedition, it is surprising how inconsiderable an armament was required. Two of the vessels were light barques, called caravels, not superior to river and coasting craft of modern days. They were built high at the prow and stern, with forecastles and cabins for the crew, but were without deck in the center. Only one of the three, called the Santa Maria, was completely decked, on board of which Columbus hoisted his flag. Martin Alonzo Pinzon commanded one of the caravels, called the Pinta, and was accompanied by his brother, Francisco Martin, as mate or pilot. The other, called the Niña, had latine sails —three-cornered sails that hang on a tree, fastened in a diagonal manner to the mast— and was commanded by Vicente Yañez Pinzon; on board of this vessel went Garcia Fernandez, the physician of Palos, in the capacity of steward. There were three other able pilots, Sancho Ruiz, Pedro Alonzo Niño, and Bartholomew Roldan, and the whole number of persons embarked was one hundred and twenty. The squadron being ready to put to sea, Columbus confessed himself to the friar Juan Perez, and partook of the communion, and his example was followed by the officers and crews, committing themselves, with the most devout and affecting ceremonials, to the especial guidance and protection of Heaven, in this perilous enterprise. A deep gloom was spread over the whole community of Palos, for almost every one had some relation or friend on board of the squadron. The spirits of the seamen, already depressed by their own fears, were still more cast down at beholding the affliction of those they left behind, who took leave of them with tears and lamentations and dismal forebodings, as of men they were never to behold again.

11

t was early in the morning of Friday, the 3rd of August, 1492, that Columbus set sail from the bar of Saltes, a small island formed by the rivers Odiel and Pinto, in front of Palos, steering for the Canary Islands, from whence he intended to strike due west. As a guide by which to sail, he had the conjectural map or chart, sent him by Paolo Toscanelli of Florence. In this it is supposed the coasts of Europe and Africa, from the south of Ireland to the end of Guinea, were delineated as immediately opposite to the extremity of Asia, while the great island of Cipango, described by Marco Polo, lay between them, fifteen hundred miles from the Asiatic coast; at this island Columbus expected first to arrive.

On the third day after setting sail, the Pinta made signal of distress, her rudder being broken and unhung. This was suspected to have been done through the contrivance of the owners, Gomez Rascon and Christoval Quintero, to disable the vessel, and cause her to be left behind. Columbus was much disturbed at this occurrence. It gave him a foretaste of the difficulties to be apprehended, from people partly enlisted on compulsion, and full of doubt and foreboding. Trivial obstacles might, in this early stage of the voyage, spread panic and mutiny through his crews, and induce them to renounce the prosecution of the enterprise.

Martin Alonzo Pinzon, who commanded the Pinta, secured the rudder with cords, but these fastenings soon gave way, and the caravel proving defective in other respects, Columbus remained three weeks cruising among the Canary Islands, in search of another vessel to replace her. Not being able to find one, the Pinta was repaired, and furnished with a new rudder. The latine sails of the Niña were also altered into square sails, that she might work more steadily and securely. While making these repairs, and taking in wood and water, Columbus was informed that three Portuguese caravels had been seen hovering off the island of Ferro. Dreading some hostile stratagem, on the part of the king of Portugal, in revenge for his having embarked in the service of Spain, he put to sea early on the morning of the 6th of September, but for three days a profound calm detained the vessels within a short distance of the land. This was a tantalizing delay, for Columbus trembled lest something should occur to defeat his expedition, and was impatient to find himself far upon the ocean, out of sight of either land or sail; which in the pure atmosphere of these latitudes may be descried at an immense distance.

On Sunday, the 9th of September, as day broke, he beheld Ferro about nine leagues distant; he was in the neighborhood, therefore, where the Portuguese caravels had been seen. Fortunately a breeze sprang up with the sun, and in the course of the day the heights of Ferro gradually faded from the horizon.

On losing sight of this last trace of land, the hearts of the crews failed them, for they seemed to have taken leave of the world. Behind them was everything dear to the heart of man—country, family, friends, life itself; before them everything was chaos, mystery, and peril. In the perturbation of the moment, they despaired of ever more seeing their homes. Many of the rugged seamen shed tears, and some broke into loud lamentations. Columbus tried in every way to soothe their distress, describing the splendid countries to which he expected to conduct them, and promising them land, riches, and everything that could arouse their cupidity or inflame their imaginations; nor were these promises made for purposes of deception, for he certainly believed he should realize them all.

He now gave orders to the commanders of the other vessels, in case they should be separated by any accident, to continue directly westward; but that after sailing seven hundred leagues, they should lay by from midnight until daylight, as at about that distance he confidently expected to find land. Foreseeing that the vague terrors already awakened among the seamen would increase with the space which intervened between them and their homes, he commenced a stratagem which he continued throughout the voyage. This was to keep two reckonings, one private, in which the true way of the ship was noted, and which he retained in secret for his own government; the other public, for general inspection, in which a number of leagues was daily subtracted from the sailings of the ships, so as to keep the crews in ignorance of the real distance they had advanced.

When about one hundred and fifty leagues west of Ferro, they fell in with part of a mast of a large vessel, and the crews, tremblingly alive to every portent, looked with a rueful eye upon this fragment of a wreck, drifting ominously at the entrance of these unknown seas.

On the 13th of September, in the evening, Columbus, for the first time, noticed the variation of the needle, a phenomenon which had never before been remarked. He at first made no mention of it, lest his people should be alarmed; but it soon attracted the attention of the pilots, and filled them with consternation. It seemed as if the very laws of Nature were changing as they advanced, and that they were entering

another world subject to unknown influences. They apprehended that the compass was about to lose its mysterious virtues, and, without this guide, what was to become of them in a vast and trackless ocean? Columbus
tasked his science and ingenuity for reasons with which
to allay their terrors. He told them that the direction of
the needle was not to the polar star, but to some fixed
and invisible point. The variation, therefore, was not
caused by any fallacy in the compass, but by the move-
ment of the north star itself, which, like the other hea-
venly bodies, had its changes and revolutions, and every
day described a circle round the pole. The high opinion they entertained of Columbus as a profound astronomer, gave weight to his theory, and their alarm
subsided.

They had now arrived within the influence of the
trade wind, which, following the sun, blows steadily
from east to west between the tropics, and sweeps over a
few adjoining degrees of the ocean. With this propitious
breeze directly aft, they were wafted gently but speedily
over a tranquil sea, so that for many days they did not
shift a sail. Columbus in his journal perpetually recurs
to the bland and temperate serenity of the weather, and
compares the pure and balmy mornings to those of
April in Andalusia, observing, that the song of the
nightingale was alone wanting to complete the illusion.

They now began to see large patches of herbs and weeds all drifting from the west. Some were such as grow about rocks or in rivers, and as green as if recently washed from the land. On one of the patches was a live crab. They saw also a white tropical bird, of a kind which never sleeps upon the sea; and tunny fish played about the ships. Columbus now supposed himself arrived in the weedy sea described by Aristotle, into which certain ships of Cadiz had been driven by an impetuous east wind.

As he advanced, there were various other signs that gave great animation to the crews, many birds were seen flying from the west; there was a cloudiness in the north, such as often hangs over land; and at sunset the imagination of the seamen, aided by their desires, would shape those clouds into distant islands. Every one was eager to be the first to behold and announce the wished-for shore; for the sovereigns had promised a pension of thirty crowns to whomsoever should first discover land. Columbus sounded occasionally with a line of two hundred fathoms (twelve hundred feet), but found no bottom. Martin Alonzo Pinzon, as well as others of his officers, and many of the seamen, were often solicitous for Columbus to alter his course, and steer in the direction of these favorable signs; but he persevered in steering to the westward, trusting that, by keeping in one steady direction, he should reach the coast of India, even if he should miss the intervening islands, and might then seek them on his return.

Notwithstanding the precaution which had been taken to keep the people ignorant of the distance they had sailed, they gradually became uneasy at the length of the voyage. The various indications of land which occasionally flattered their hopes, passed away one after another, and the same interminable expanse of sea and sky continued to extend before them. They had advanced much farther to the west than ever man had sailed before, and though already beyond the reach of succor, were still pressing onward and onward into that apparently boundless abyss. Even the favorable wind, which seemed as if providentially sent to waft them to the New World with such bland and gentle breezes, was conjured by their fears into a source of alarm. They feared that the wind in these seas always prevailed from the east, and if so, would never permit their return to Spain. A few light breezes from the west allayed for a time their last apprehension, and several small birds, such as keep about groves and orchards, came singing in the morning, and flew away at night. Their song was wonderfully cheering to the hearts of the poor mariners, who hailed it as the voice of land. The birds they had hitherto seen had been large and strong of wing; but such small birds, they observed, were too feeble to fly far, and their singing showed that they were not exhausted by their flight.

On the following day there was a profound calm, and the sea, as far as the eye could reach, was covered with weeds, so as to have the appearance of a vast inundated meadow, a phenomenon attributed to the immense quantities of submarine plants which are detached by the currents from the bottom of the ocean. The seamen now feared that the sea was growing shallow; they dreaded lurking rocks, and shoals, and quicksands, and that their vessels might run aground, as it were, in the midst of the ocean, far out of the track of human aid, and with no shore where the crews could take refuge. Columbus proved the fallacy of this alarm, by sounding with a deep sealine, and finding no bottom.

For three days there was a continuance of light summer airs, from the southward and westward, and the sea was as smooth as a mirror. The crews now became uneasy at the calmness of the weather. They observed that the contrary winds they experienced were transient and unsteady, and so light as not to ruffle the surface of the sea, the only winds of constancy and force were from the west, and even those had not power to disturb the torpid stillness of the ocean: there was a risk, therefore, either of perishing amidst stagnant and shoreless waters, or of being prevented, by contrary winds, from ever returning to their native country.

Columbus continued, with admirable patience, to reason with these absurd fancies, but in vain; when fortunately there came on a heavy swell of the sea, unaccompanied by wind, a phenomenon that often occurs in the broad ocean, caused by the impulse of some past gale, or distant current of wind. It was, nevertheless, regarded with astonishment by the mariners, and dispelled the imaginary terrors occasioned by the calm.

The situation of Columbus was daily becoming more and more critical. The impatience of the seamen rose to absolute mutiny. They gathered together in the retired parts of the ships, at first in little knots of two and three, which gradually increased and became formidable, joining in murmurs and menaces against the admiral. They exclaimed against him as an ambitious desperado, who, in a mad phantasy, had determined to do something extravagant to render himself notorious. What obligation bound them to persist, or when were the terms of their agreement to be considered as fulfilled? They had already penetrated into seas untraversed by a sail, and where man had never before adventured. Were they to sail on until they should perish, or until all return with their frail ships should become impossible? Who would blame them should they consult their safety and return? The admiral was a foreigner, without friends or influence. His scheme had been condemned by the learned as idle and visionary, and discountenanced by people of all ranks. There was, there-fore, no party on his side, but rather a large number who would be gratified by his failure.

Such are some of the reasonings by which these men prepared themselves for open rebellion. Some even proposed, as an effectual mode of silencing all after-complaints of the admiral, that they should throw him into the sea, and give out that he had fallen overboard, while contemplating the stars and signs of the heavens, with his astronomical instruments.

Columbus was not ignorant of these secret cabals, but he kept a serene and steady countenance, soothing some with gentle words, stimulating the pride or the av-arice of others, and openly menacing the most refracto-ry with punishment. New hopes diverted them for a time. On the 25th of September, Martin Alonzo Pinzon mounted on the stern of his vessel, and shouted, "Land! land! Señor, I claim the reward!" There was, indeed, such an appearance of land in the southwest, that Co-lumbus threw himself upon his knees, and returned thanks to God, and all the crews joined in chanting *Gloria in excelcis* ("Glory be to God on high"). The ships al-tered their course, and stood all night to the southwest, but the morning light put an end to all their hopes as to a dream: the fancied land proved to be nothing but an evening cloud, and had vanished in the night.

For several days, they continued on with alternate hopes and murmurs, until the various signs of land became so numerous, that the seamen, from a state of despondency, passed to one of high excitement. Eager to obtain the promised pension, they were continually giving the cry of land; until Columbus declared, that should any one give a notice of the kind, and land not be discovered within three days afterwards, he should thenceforth forfeit all claim of the reward.

On the 7th of October, they had come seven hundred and fifty leagues, the distance at which Columbus had computed to find the island of Cipango. There were great flights of small field birds to the southwest, which seemed to indicate some neighboring land in that direction, where they were sure of food and a resting place. Yielding to the solicitations of Martin Alonzo Pinzon and his brothers, Columbus, on the evening of the 7th, altered his course, therefore to the westsouthwest. As he advanced, the signs of land increased; the birds came singing about the ships; and herbage floated by as fresh and green as if recently from shore. When, however, on the evening of the third day of this new course, the seamen beheld the sun go down upon a shoreless horizon, they again broke forth into loud clamors, and insisted upon abandoning the voyage. Columbus endeavored to pacify them by gentle words and liberal promises; but finding these only increased their violence, he assumed a different tone, and told them it was useless to murmur; the expedition had been sent by the sovereigns to seek the Indies, and happen what might, he was determined to persevere, until, by the blessing of God, he should accomplish the enterprise.

He was now at open defiance with his crew, and his situation would have been desperate, but, fortunately, the manifestations of land on the following day were such as no longer to admit of doubt. A green fish, such as keeps about rocks, swam by the ships; and a branch of thorn, with berries on it, floated by; they picked up, also, a reed, a small board, and, above all, a staff artificially carved. All gloom and murmuring was now at an end, and throughout the day each one was on the watch for the long-sought land.

In the evening, when, according to custom, the mariners had sung the *salve regina*, or vesper hymn to the Virgin, Columbus made an impressive address to his crew, pointing out the goodness of God in thus conducting them by soft and favoring breezes across a tranquil ocean to the promised land. He expressed a strong confidence of making land that every night, and ordered that a vigilant lookout should be kept from the forecastle, promising to whomsoever should make the discovery, a doublet of velvet, in addition to the pension to be given by the sovereigns.

The breeze had been fresh all day, with more sea than usual; at sunset they stood again to the west, and were ploughing the waves at a rapid rate, the Pinta keeping the lead from his superior sailing. The greatest animation prevailed throughout the ships; not an eye was closed that night. As the evening darkened, Columbus took his station on the top of the castle or cabin on the high poop of his vessel. However he might carry a cheerful and confident countenance during the day, it was to him a time of the most painful anxiety; and now then he was wrapped from observation by the shades of night, he maintained an intense and unremitting watch, ranging his eye along the dusky horizon, in search of the most vague indications of land. Suddenly, about ten o'clock he thought he beheld a light glimmering at a distance. Fearing that his eager hopes might deceive him, he called Pedro Gutierrez, a gentleman of the king's bedchamber, and demanded whether he saw a light in that direction; the latter replied in the affirmative. Columbus, yet doubtful whether it might not be some delusion of the fancy, called Rodrigo Sanchez of Segovia, and made the same inquiry. By the time the latter had ascended the round-house, the light had disappeared. They saw it once or twice afterwards in sudden and passing gleams, as it it were a torch in the bark of a fisherman, rising and sinking with the waves; or in the hands of some person on shore, borne up and down as he walked from house to house. So transient and uncer-

tain were these gleams, that few attached any importance to them; Columbus, however, considered them as
certain signs of land, and, moreover, that the land was
inhabited.

They continued on their course until two in the
morning, when a gun from the Pinta gave the joyful signal of land. It was first discovered by a mariner named
Rodriguez Bermejo, resident of Triana, a suburb of Seville, but native of Alcala de la Guadaira; but the reward
was afterwards adjudged to the Admiral, for having previously perceived the light. The land was now clearly
seen about two leagues distant, whereupon they took in
sail, and laid to, waiting impatiently for the dawn.

The thoughts and feelings of Columbus in this little
space of time must have been tumultuous and intense.
At length, in spite of every difficulty and danger, he had
accomplished his object. The great mystery of the ocean
was revealed; his theory, which had been the scoff of
sages, was triumphantly established; he had secured to
himself a glory which must be as durable as the world
itself.

It is difficult even for the imagination to conceive the
feelings of such a man, at the moment of so sublime a
discovery. What a bewildering crowd of conjectures
must have thronged upon his mind, as to the land
which lay before him, covered with darkness! That it
was fruitful was evident from the vegetables which float-

ed from its shores. He thought, too, that he perceived in the balmy air the fragrance of aromatic groves. The moving light which he had beheld, proved that it was the residence of man. But what were its inhabitants? Were they like those of other parts of the globe; or were they some strange and monstrous race, such as the imagination in those times was prone to give to all remote and unknown regions? Had he come upon some wild island, far in the Indian seas; or was this the famed Cipango itself, the object of his golden fancies? A thousand speculations of the kind must have swarmed upon him, as he watched for the night to pass away; wondering whether the morning light would reveal a savage wilderness, or dawn upon spicy groves, and glittering fanes, and gilded cities, and all the splendors of oriental civilization.

When the day dawned, Columbus saw before him a level and beautiful island, several leagues in extent, of great freshness and verdure, and covered with trees like a continual orchard. Though everything appeared in the wild luxuriance of untamed nature yet the island was evidently populous, for the inhabitants were seen issuing from the woods, and running from all parts to the shore. They were all perfectly naked, and, from their attitudes and gestures, appeared lost in astonishment at the sight of the ships. Columbus made signal to cast anchor, and to man the boats. He entered his own boat, richly attired in scarlet, and bearing the royal standard. Martin Alonzo Pinzon, and Vicente Yañez his brother, likewise put off in their boats, each bearing the banner of the enterprise, emblazoned with a green cross, having, on each side, the letters F and Y, surmounted by crowns, the Spanish initials of the Castilian monarchs, Fernando and Ysabel.

THE END

Footnotes

1. Idrisi (1100-1166), also Sharif Al Idrisi, was the most famous Arab geographer in the Middle Ages. A descendant of the Prophet Mohammed and son of princes of Malaga, Idrisi was born in Ceuta, studied in Cordova and was commissioned by Roger II, King of Sicily, to make a map of the known world. Idrisi completed his work in 1154, a silver globe and planishpere, based, in part on his own writings (a book entitled *Delights on Him Who Would Traverse the World)* and on the work of Ptolemy. Idrisi's was the most complete Islamic map of his time and the most exact of the Mediterranean coast and the near east.

2. The houses of Anjou and of Aragon fought each other for nearly two centuries over the Italian kingdoms of Naples and Sicily.

3. Henry the Navigator (1394-1460), King of Portugal, sponsored the most important explorations of the coast of Africa during the XV century, which reached as far as present day Sierra Leone. His work laid the foun-

dation for the great expansion of Europe in the XVI century.

4. Paulo Toscanelli (1397-1482), Florentine geographer who sustained the theory that the world was round and could be circumnavigated. The map Toscanelli sent to Columbus in 1474 has been lost.

5. In the Middle Ages Europeans gave to Japan the name of Cipango and to China the names of Cathay and Mangi. During the time of Columbus Europeans were not sure that Cathay, China and Mangi were one and the same country, that is today's China. Mangi, in fact, was the ancient chinese name for the people south of the Yangtse river and was used by the Mongols to refer to south China.

6. Ptolemy (Greek, flourished 2nd century A.D.) One of the most celebrated astronomers, geographers and mathematicians of antiquity. His work, which exerted enormous influence on knowledge for over 1200 years, was collected in two great books, *The Great Astronomer* (known also as *The Almagest*) and his *Guide to Geography*. Ptolemy believed that the earth was the center of the universe and all other celestial bodies revolved around it.

7. Marco Polo (1254-1324) was a Venetian who became famous for his travels through China and for his personal and commercial relationships with the Chi-

nese Emperor, the great Kublai Khan. The Polo brothers, (the father Nicolo and the uncle Maffeo) had been
the first Europeans to meet the Great Khan.

8. Antilla was a legendary island in the Atlantic, also
known as the Island of the Seven Cities, and it appears
in most of the maps of the XV century. In his letter to
Columbus of 1474 Toscanelli takes Antilla as the principal landmark for measuring the distance between Lisbon and Cipango (Japan). After the discovery of the
West Indies by Columbus, the Spanish term Antillas was
commonly used to designate the new lands.

9. Tartary, an area of Asia, home of the Russian Tar-
tars of today.

10. John II was King of Portugal from 1481 to 1495.
In 1488 one of his navigators, Bartholomeu Diaz round-
ed the Cape of Good Hope and reached the coast of
East Africa. Diaz returned to Lisbon in 1492 to be greet-
ed with the surprising news of Columbus's discovery of
the Indies.

11. Martin Behaim was a German astronomer who
worked as map maker for the Casa da India in Lisbon.
Just a few months before Columbus landed in the new
world Behaim made a globe, the oldest terrestrial globe
in existence. On it the western coast of Europe and the
east coast of Asia face each other across the waters of
the Atlantic.

Cartography and discoveries were state secrets in the 15th and 16th centuries. Map making, mostly in the form of compass charts, flourished in the Italian ports, especially Genoa, Ancona and Venice. On these charts the Portuguese recorded their voyages along the coasts of Africa. By the end of the 15th century the Casa da India at Lisbon was training highly skilled pilots and map makers. Portuguese authorities tried to keep secret their discoveries and routes and there was no end to the intrigues by the other European potentates to get their hands on these Portuguese maps and charts.

12. Fernando (1452-1516) and Isabella (1451-1504), also written Ysabel in old Spanish, were married in 1474, uniting their respective reigns of Aragon and Castile. They became known as the "Catholic Kings" of Spain, bringing about the unity of all the independent kingdoms of Spain under one shared monarchy.

13. Pedro Gonzalez de Mendoza (1428-1494) was a powerful prelate of the Catholic Church in Spain, had been Chancellor to Henry IV of Castile and became the personal adviser to Queen Isabella.

14. Lactantius (250-330), born in Africa, wrote *Divine Institutions*, the first attempt at a systematic presentation of Christian thought in the Latin language.

15. St. Augustine (354-430) was born in Tagaste in Roman Africa (modern day Algeria). He is considered

the greatest thinker of Christian antiquity and in his own day was recognized as the dominant figure of the Western Church. His most famous work is his *Confessions*, the story of his stormy life and conversion to Catholicism.

16. El Zagal was pretender to the throne of the Moorish Kingdom of Granada. He was the brother of the rightful king, the Sultan Muley Hassan, who was overthrown by his own son Boabdil el Chico. Later, El Zagal usurped Boabdil's throne and during a few years led a civil war against him which contributed to the downfall of Granada and its final surrender to the Catholic Kings.

17. The Grand Sultan of Egypt at this time was a member of the Mameluke dynasty of Islamic sovereigns who ruled Egypt and Jerusalem from 1247 to 1517.

18. Boabdil ruled from 1482 to 1492 as the King of Granada, the last Moorish Kingdom of Islamic Spain. He had been proclaimed sultan by popular revolt in 1482 in favor of his father, Muley Hassan. In 1483 he was taken prisoner by the Castilians and was released after a secret agreement that he would surrender Granada upon demand by the Catholic Kings. In 1491 Ferdinand and Isabella summoned Boabdil to fulfill his promise, and on his refusal they sieged the city, which fell to them on January 2, 1492. Boabdil went to Africa, settled in Fez and died in battle in 1527.

19. Khan means "sovereign" in Mongol. As of the reigns of Ghengis Khan and Kublai Khan Europeans used the term to refer to the emperors of China, who almost indistinctly became known as the Grand Khans. During the time of Columbus the Grand Khan was, in fact, Dayan Khan, emperor of Mongolia, while the emperor of China was a member of the Ming Dynasty, Chu Yu-t'ang.

Alana and the ...

AIHBER KHAN

ACKNOWLEDGEMENTS

Hi, I'm Aihber Khan. I was nine when I started working on this book. But when I started Alana and the ..., I never thought that I would have to thank so many people who raised me, taught me and inspired me with their care, attention and wisdom.

First of all, I would like to thank from the depth of my heart and soul, my truly wonderful family: My Mom for motivating me to write this book and giving hope every single day. Without her I wouldn't be able to get this book done. She's not only my Mom, she's my best friend. Next, I want to thank my Dad for helping me find a publisher for this book and kept pushing me forward to be courageous, believe in my academic goals and live happily without worries. Now, I want to thank my cutest sister, Akaisha. She makes me laugh, shares with me, and she's always happy of my achievements. She's my heart!

I'm so lucky to have such amazing Grandparents, who gave me so much love that I can't thank them enough for their affection. They are always proud of me.

And now these are some of the mentors who provided the education and wisdom, I will always cherish:

I'll begin by mentioning my greatest Principal ever: Mrs. Werner! She is very helpful; and I love to be on her list of Principal's Honor Roll! And of course, the best and funniest Vice Principal ever: Mr. Scott.

And now a big thanks to my music, art, media, guidance, computer, and many teachers throughout these years: Mr. Winters, Mr. Shea, Ms. Aisner, Mrs. Nadrowski, Mrs. Almeida, Ms. Stokkers, Ms. Spanier, Ms. Chenoweth, Ms. Donna, and funny Ms. Jenny.

And now, I'll start by thanking, my pre-K teachers, who helped me getting started academically; my Kindergarten teacher: Mrs. Armas; my second grade teachers: Mrs. Carroll and Mrs. Buettin; third grade teachers: Mrs. Shultz, Mrs. Mathews and Mrs. Whitman; and fourth grade teacher, Mrs. Keisel. Last but certainly not least, my fifth grade teachers: Ms. Smith; sweetest Mrs. Innerst; kindest Mr. Anderson; and my wonderful homeroom teacher, Mr. Tomasiello. Last but certainly not least, my chess teacher, Mrs. Antolik.

In conclusion, thank you everyone for all your inspiration and love. I really appreciate it! I hope you like my book. Thank you oh, so, very much!

———ฅฅฅฅฅฅ————

TABLE OF CONTENTS

CHAPTER I

NEW YORK

I t's going to be great! My dad just got us tickets to New York. I couldn't wait. Mom and Dad were planning for quite some time — and at last we were going because of my Dad's *National Medical Seminar* — for a week or two. We first visited New York, when I was five; I barely remember that experience. But this time, I'm going to have a blast!

"Start packing, girls; we're leaving tomorrow!" Mom said.

When I got to my room and started packing, I took almost my whole room. I took clothes, toys, and lots of video games. As I looked out of the window it was dark and it was time to go to bed. I said Goodnight to my parents and my little sister, Melody, then went to bed. I was extremely tired and slept like a baby.

"Rise and shine, Honey," when my mom woke me up in the morning, it was time to leave!

"Woo, Hoo!" I yelled.

I put my clothes on—almost forgot to brush my teeth, then got all my stuff, and got in the car to endure an hour drive to the airport.

At last we got to the airport. At the check-in counter, a petite lady, took our passports and luggage. I noticed her because she was too petite; I mean like someone put clothes on a skeleton. As

I always say, *be skinny but never bony.* I'm just kidding; I never say that. Well, moving on … we got to the security checkpoint, were cleared, and ready to go.

There was a huge rush of people. Through the glass window, Melody and I enjoyed watching the planes, take-off and landing.

In a few minutes there was an announcement:

"Memorable Airlines Flight 13 is now ready for boarding at the Gate A. We request passengers to please have your passports and boarding cards ready."

Boy, what an unlucky number! I thought.

Everyone rushed into the line. We were in the business class.

"I'm thirsty," Melody whined as she sat in her seat and pretended fastening her seat belt just for fun.

As the plane took off, I started reading a mystery book. This was a four hour flight to New York. Melody started going here and there; which I think the flight attendant was not very happy about. Mom was keeping an eye on Melody, while knitting. My Dad was busy doing business paperwork. The best part was when we got unique snacks that were different from any other flight I've ever travelled.

This was not my first time travelling; but this time, I had a weird hunch. I can't clearly explain — but I couldn't shake the feeling that — I would have a notable time. I hope my feeling doesn't deceive me. Fingers crossed!

"Ah ... *finally*," I saw the plane landing at the

JFK International Airport. Until my family carried the bags from the top compartment, I ran outside in happiness! I saw my family still coming out, slowly.

"*Please* ... come out, faster!" I begged them.

After Customs and Immigration, we went out and saw my Dad's associate, Mr. Tomasiello. He was waiting for us.

"Oh, my," I gasped as I saw a limo waiting for us.

"How was your trip, little ladies?" Mr. Tomasiello asked us in a childish manner.

"UH ... good," I said annoyingly.

"Velly, velly, good!" Melody said in her jolly and stammering lingo.

Finally we entered the hotel and got a suite.

"Can I go out exploring?" I asked my parents.

Mom replied, "Yes, you can! But come back on time for supper."

"Okay, Mom," I replied, then went out.

I saw hundreds of people, restaurants, buildings, and parks too. I felt like everyone had their lights on. It was so bright!

CHAPTER II

LOST!

I n a few minutes of looking around, I felt so sleepy. I wanted to go back to the suite. I tried to find my way back, but I found out I was LOST! I was terrified thinking about what would happen.

"What do I do?" I asked myself.

I remembered what my Dad told me. "Never talk to strangers unless you know that they work there and cops, of course. It is most important to keep yourself safe."

I decided to follow his advice. But I couldn't tell who to trust? There were people walking everywhere. I couldn't spot any cop. I would go into the restaurants but those were too jammed. Questions started floating in my mind: *am I lost forever? Where should I go? Will I ever see my family again? Will I ever ...?* The questions were silly but they started freaking me out.

CHAPTER III

THE STRANGE GIRL

"Hello there!"

As I was about to ask myself another question, suddenly there was a voice behind me. I turned around and there was a girl. She looked unreal, pale — like she hasn't eaten in years. I didn't know her so I said nothing, and walked away because, she was a stranger. Well, at least to me. As I walked away I felt a cool breeze behind me. I turned around again, and realized she was following me.

I stopped, sighed, and then said, "Ok you stopped me; you win. What is your name?"

"Lizzy," she replied.

There was a cool breeze as she talked.

"And what's yours?" she asked.

I can't tell a complete stranger my name. But I thought … *what can a petite, harmless girl do to me?*

"Alana," I replied.

As I heard Lizzy's name in my mind a few times, I realized that it sounded very familiar. While talking and walking with her, I remembered where my hotel was.

"I have to go … bye," I said.

Lizzy said, "Okay. I will be here to see you

again."

Well I wouldn't be! I thought mockingly.

I was at the hotel before I knew it. My mom opened the door of the room. I noticed mixed wrinkles of concern and anger, on her forehead. She let me come in without saying a word; maybe thinking that I must be tired.

Dad and Melody were already sound asleep. I got into bed without supper. I was too tired to even have a bite of my mom's delicious supper. She cooks everywhere, even when we are in hotels. Most people order room service or eat a buffet. Nope, she tries her best to keep us healthy with her nutritious cooking.

I think, in a few minutes I was sound asleep, too. I know, out of the whole family I was the most exhausted one.

CHAPTER IV

LIZZY'S VISIT

A s the sun slowly came up and the sky became a light shade of orange and pink I woke excitedly for another day of fun!

I don't know why but I wondered if Lizzy was still there. As I looked out the window I was amazed. She was out there sitting on a bench near the fountain. I realized she was not kidding when she said she would be waiting here for me, but I also realized one more thing, our room was on the first floor and my door was right in front of the fountain.

She was too creepy. I didn't want to see her again. As I shook my thoughts, she was gone. Where? How? I wondered because I did not see her leaving.

Oh well. I thought. *Why should I waste a perfect day worrying about her?* I got busy with my family.

"Dadum, can we go to the museum? I heard it's really admirable," I convinced him.

I knew he was too busy in his meetings but I tried.

"Alana dear, you have a way with words!" he smiled. "I'm not that busy today, so tell your mom and little sis to get ready!" he patted my head.

"O, Mommy dearest!!" I ran to her. "Guess where we are going?"

"To a park?" Melody interrupted while combing her doll's hair.

"No, silly. Why would we go to the park when we are in a new city and there are many more places to explore?" I asked her intelligently.

"I don't get it," Melody said innocently.

"Well, don't think too much," I tapped her head, sarcastically.

"Okay. Tell already," Mom was fed up with our arguing.

"*Museum*, here we come!" I said in a deep voice.

The museum was fascinating; specially the art from ancient Egypt. After the museum, we went to the zoo.

"Oo, oo ... ah, ah," Melody imitated a monkey. "Monkeys are my favorite animals!"

"Good choice, Melody!" once again I said, sarcastically.

At the end of the day, we sat in a fancy restaurant to have a scrumptious dinner.

"Ah," Melody sighed as we entered our room.

She was not the only one. After a hectic but fulfilled day, we were fast asleep, snoring and drooling—Dadum snores, and Melody drools. I usually just sleep tight and smile with sweet dreams. Unfortunately, tonight was no sweet dream but a bitter nightmare:

"I'm coming for you, Alana!" the eerie girl said. "I killed a few while waiting for you. Then you were born. And I had to wait a little more until you are about the right age to be killed. So it's time to die, ALANA!"

"No ... please don't!" I woke up fearful.

"Honey!" Dadum came running in my room. "It's okay. It was just a nightmare!" Dadum assured me but I was not okay.

"It was sad. She fell ... it was dark ... a hollow ditch ..."

"Who will, sweetie?" Dadum was worried.

"The girl ... in my nightmare — I had this nightmare before. I don't know when but I am sure, I had it before, Dadum," I was curious.

"Alana, it was just a dream. No one can hurt my baby!" Dadum hugged me and stayed with me until I slept.

The next morning, I was not scared of that nightmare. But I was curious about Lizzy. Is she outside, waiting for me? I had to look.

Yup. There you are! I saw her. *Should I tell Mom and Dad? Nope. I can handle her, myself! Right?* My thoughts were mixed up, fighting to find answers.

How will I get rid of her? I can't believe I was saying this but I can't wait till we get out of New York. She made me have nightmares.

I decided to have a talk with that Lizzy person.

As I went out to the door — touched the doorknob—and was about to sneak out, there was a knock on the door. Wondering who it was, I opened the door and saw Lizzy, standing right in front of me. She was wearing a pearl necklace, a pair of earrings, jeans, a red shirt and sandals. Lizzy seemed spoiled and rich. She was pretty but her face looked even paler in the morning.

"How did you find my hotel room?" I asked her suspiciously.

"I followed you," she said in a breezy voice. "I saw your hotel number then waited till morning to meet you."

I was confused for a moment then asked her, "How did you follow me? I looked behind me before I entered my room. It was almost like you were invisible."

"Oh, I have my ways," she sounded like she

was hiding something.

But no worries. My name is *ALANA*, and I'm really good at solving mysteries. I was going to find out. I also wondered why she kept spying on me. I told her to come in even though I didn't want her to. I was hoping she would say no thank you I am busy but instead she said thank you, and came in. Well, at least she had manners.

CHAPTER V

THE CLUES

L izzy walked in a weird way almost like she was floating. She asked me to hold the doors that were in her way, saying — she couldn't touch anything because she was sick. But I didn't believe any word because if she was that sick, why would she come to me. It was not that urgent to meet someone you just knew for a day! *I don't think so, Missy!*

"Let me introduce you to my parents," I thought my parent should at least know her, in case she's a villain and is here to kidnap me — they can tell the cops what she looked like. My hobby of collecting mysterious souvenirs and suspenseful books has made my brain think like a suspicious person. But it's useful most of the times.

"No, thanks. I'm very shy!" Lizzy said. "Let's just go out," she tried to be friendly.

"Um ... where?" I asked. But I didn't care where we were going. I really wanted to find out who she is? Where she lives? And the only way to find answers was to go with her.

"Come. Let me just tell my parents," I pulled her to come with me.

"No. I'll be outside," she left my hand and went outside.

Clever girl! I thought.

We went to a park. It was jam-packed because of Saturday night. Some were having a picnic and some were walking their dogs.

"It's too crowded. I have to go," Lizzy said annoyingly.

"What?" I was surprised. "We walked all the way, and now you want to leave?"

"We will come next time ... when the park is empty," Lizzy said smiling.

"Okey-dokey?" I was confused. Why does she want the park to be empty?

"Bye," I said as she left. But you know me, I'm more curious than *Curious George*. So I followed.

She was going in the windy, dark woods. I looked up at the trees and there was a sign. It said CEMETERY! I gasped.

"Why was she going into the cemetery?" I was scared to go in, but I had to find out what she was doing. My body was shaking in fright. It was the darkest night ever. The owls were hooting; I felt the trees swaying rowdily from the push of the rough breeze. Suddenly it was freezing. I swear I could hear someone chanting my name:

ALANA.

It was too dark, I could barely see Lizzy. As I moved ahead, I saw hundreds of graves.

Lizzy disappeared as I looked — I couldn't find her anywhere in sight. I cancelled my plan to follow her. As I turned back, I was about to trip over a tombstone.

Why did I come here? I have never been this petrified in my life. This experience is overwhelming.

CHAPTER VI

STAYING

My steps were way ahead of me. I was rushing to the hotel.

I'm sure; her house must be behind the cemetery. That must be a short cut. I calmed myself thinking of a perfectly good explanation behind all this.

Okay, I am going to forget all about this ... just go to the suite and get a good night's sleep. I persuaded myself.

As I walked on the red brick pathway, I looked up at the stars glowing down at me … I begged them to make this *bad* stuff stop. I reached the hotel suite — the door was open. Mom must have left it open for me. I opened the door — it creaked open … it felt like, I was in a horror movie because it was creepy that the door creaked open, but I didn't worry about it and went to my bedroom. I didn't change, and hid under my blanket to feel safe. I heard Mom came to check on me, but I was not in the mood to tell her my foolishness. It was just eight o'clock, but I just had to sleep — to erase the incident from my memory.

I woke up with the sound of my sister yelling, "Wake up, Alana!"

I was beat, but still got out of bed — changed and went to the other room. I saw my dad sitting on the couch and smiling. He said he had great news.

Oh no. Whenever he says it is good news, it's usually bad news for me.

He said, "We are getting a house and …" he tried to surprise us with a long pause after the word *AND*, "we're buying a house and moving here! What do you think, huh?" Dadum waited for a jolly response. He received it, but not from me.

"Wow, John … it sounds just right!" Mom hugged Melody.

Melody freed herself from Mom's tight hug, and jumped into Dadum's arms. "Daddy, I want to see the new house!"

"Very soon, Melo! Very soon," Dadum kissed her, and then looked at my dropped face. "Anything you want to share, Alana?"

What could I say—all of my dreams were crushed. "It was just a trip but now we are going to live here?" I yelled.

Everyone stared at me.

"Do we *have* to stay here?" I controlled my anger.

"Sorry, but I already decided to open my practice here, with Tomasiello," he sat beside me and told his plans. "It's a perfect opportunity—I found a great town—an astounding house and decent schools," he continued. "It's time to settle, Honey! Traveling is fun and we'll definitely continue it but let's take a break for a while and create a home of our choice! Am I Right?"

I didn't answer. I was too upset.

"And besides, your room is the *biggest*," he

tried again to make me happy.

I can't stay angry with Dadum. "It'll be fine ... I guess."

"That's my girl!" he hugged me, and said, "We are going to move in two days. I'm going to go to the front office and inform them. So ... let's get ready guys! Chop, chop!"

"Just great, I have to pack up again! Peachy!" I made a face.

"Watch your tone, Miranda!" Mom said in her usual polite, but guiding way.

My heart was sunken down. I went to my bedroom and started packing up. While I was packing I started thinking—*it wouldn't be that bad. I mean it might be in a breathtaking, friendly neighborhood with girls of my age. Our home might be under the beauti-*

ful trees, and have the greenest backyard; and maybe a chimney for Santa, who can bring gifts for Melody. It might also have bricks with cool handprints of little children; no wait, that's a preschool, I'm confused with.

And best of all — I'm going far away from Lizzy. She will not know my new address!

Once I lost my train of thoughts, I was done, packing. I actually felt a little excited about seeing the house, and if it had the stuff I dreamt about, it'll be picture-perfect!

I don't know why, but I needed to see Lizzy just one last time. It'll remove my suspicions about her being bizarre and I'll be ready to move calmly. The next morning I asked Mom, "I'm done packing. Is it okay if I go out?"

"Yeah … but come soon. You have to help me pack Melody's stuff," Mom ordered.

"Aw … why can't she help you? Why me?" I don't like packing at all; especially Melody's billion of jeans, plenty of princess books, and millions of socks. Yup she loves socks more than anything useful in the world.

"She's your little sis! *Remember?*" Mom smiled.

"Fine!" I went out.

It was dusk; not too many people were in the park. Somehow I knew Lizzy would be here. I looked around — sat on a bench for a while, then walked near the lake, but no sign of Lizzy.

Soon it was night. The street lamps were dim.

"That's it. I'm leaving," I was frustrated. I don't like waiting.

"Looking for me?" as I turned, Lizzy appeared out of nowhere.

"Hi … where did you come from?" I asked.

"From there, silly," she pointed to the road.

"I … just came to say bye. I'm moving," why did I have to tell her?

"Oh, okay … where?" She asked curiously.

"Nowhere … just somewhere my Dad's opening a practice … there … so … nowhere," I was not making any sense. I was trying to hide our actual location from her, but I have no idea why I came in the first place. It was like — I was pulled towards her.

"I'll come by to say hi!" she was not worried — as if she knew where I was going.

"Ah. I love the night," Lizzy said looking at the stars. "I just love looking at the moon in the dark, and I love the breeze whistling through the trees. Oh, I just love the crickets chirping in the silent night ..."

"Wow, you sure love the night," I mocked with a smile.

"I am SERIOUS!" Lizzy replied madly.

Oh, boy! Red alert! I thought.

I should be careful. Well, I was silly enough to go with a stranger and now *be careful?* I must be out of my mind!

"I got to go. Mom must be waiting," I tried to find my way out.

"You are not going anywhere," Lizzy's voice

changed from friendly to villainous.

But she recovered quickly. "I mean, you haven't seen the *'Famished Forest'*, yet," she said in a furtive voice.

"Famished Forest?" I was puzzled. "What in the world is that?" I knew she was buying more time to spend with me. But why?

Maybe she's an orphan. No friends or family. She's looking for a best a friend. I was feeling sad as I created my own weird answers, in my mind.

Well, no harm in finding what she's talking about. "So where is this, *Famished Forest* of yours?" I asked.

"It is said," she started, "that the forest appears when it's hungry for more blood."

As she started telling me the story of that for-est, it felt as if — it was happening right in front of me — like some horror, suspense movie ... playing in front of my shocked eyes.

"... One unfortunate day, four very dear friends, went on a camping trip, in the *Mountains of Arama* ..."

Yes ... I could *see* and *hear* them like my sixth sense just woke up in the worst nightmare of my life. It was happening, right in front of me. That unfortunate day, was being recreated for me:

"Nick, please tell me — you didn't forget it!" Rob was worried.

"No big deal ... we can cut some wood, make a bonfire, and camp right here. We can continue later — in the *bright* light of a *sweet* morning," Nick told a solution in his own careless, hilarious nature.

But no one was in a laughing mood, because of their tiring hike through Arama Mountains.

"What a brilliant idea! Are we using our carving knives to cut *some* wood?" Rob was sarcastic because they were not carrying axes.

"So we just use phone lights and moonlight, for now!" Demitry said angrily. "And tell me Nick — how in the *world*, this forest was not on the map?"

"It appears, magically to annoy few friends!" Nick was still comical.

Rob was about to punch him, when Murray came between them,

"Guys, guys, relax! No need for a feud. We are here to have the best time of our lives. Don't ruin it!"

"Sorry, guys!" Nick apologized realizing Murray is right. They planned for this trip for a couple of months now.

Demitry jumped in. "It's an honest mistake. We had too many bags, so it was hard to keep track of the one with the flashlights and lanterns — the most important bag," Demitry said sarcastically and everyone giggled.

"Okay, *Okay*," Murray tried to calm them. "Let's not spoil our amazing hike and a great swim in the lake."

"I agree," Rob said controlling his temper.

"Let's see some fire, guys!" Demitry ordered.

They collected twigs, leaves and whatever they could without any ax or any light.

Out of nowhere, Nick found a ditch that made no sense. "Hey, over here!" he hollered.

"What is this?" Murray said puzzled.

They shined the cell phone's lights on it. The ditch was completely round, like three-sixty degree, accurate circle. Very deep like a well, with burned yellowish grass around it.

"This is creepy! When did you dig this?" Demitry touched nick's shoulder in a mocking way.

"It is not funny!" Nick was suddenly angry as if he doesn't want anyone to insult the ditch. "I heard this deep hole has special powers," Nick explained.

"When did you hear that?" Rob questioned.

"The last time I came with a few friends," Nick said

"What friends? We never came here with you. And as far as I know we are your only friends who can put up with you," Rob teased.

But Nick was not laughing, "I came with them, 50 years ago." Nick was unemotional.

"Yeah, right. Trying to scare us with your weird face," Demitry said looking at Nick's blank face.

"So you are not twenty-five but seventy-five?" Rob scoffed.

"Yes!" Nick replied,

"Will you please stop this nonsense" Murray had enough, "let's go!" he touched Nick's shoulder.

"No one is going anywhere. I wanted you here. That's why the forest became visible. As planned,

I didn't bring lights because where you are going … you don't need to see anything – but feel!" Nick was mysterious.

It was not funny anymore.

"ENOUGH," Rob said irately, fed up with Nick's absurd joke.

But it was too late. Nick's eyes turned red as lava, his feet left the ground. His body turned white. Rob, Murray and Demitry were hysterical and fearful.

"Oh, jeez!" Murray understood something was definitely not right.

"What's happening?" Rob asked shaking.

"He's not our Nick – but someone else!" Demitry realized they were in danger. "RUN!" he yelled.

But it was too late. The funny, shy, friendly Nick was not himself. Was he possessed? Was he a spirit or ghost? Was he like this as long as they've known him? They could only imagine.

No second chances for answers.

Screams spread in the midst of a deceiving night. Their dream trip turned into nightmare — and not long, they were pulled into the hole, as if the pit was a quicksand. No one could hear their cries or pull them to rescue.

Three best friends vanished in the vortex and the forest was called *Famished Forest*, for gulping whenever it needs some fresh screams for revenge.

"Ah ... where am I?" Nick woke up from sunlight shining on his face. He was lying down on a rough ground with no sign of any forest or pit as far as he can see.

"No ... where ... my friends!?" his sympathetic heart was shedding blood tears.

"Robby ... Demitry ... Murray ... my friends!" He called but no one was there to explain to him — whether it was just a bad dream, or shocking reality. He couldn't figure out what went through the horrific night. But he remembered vaguely — something entering his soul, after he found the ditch. It was a spirit of a girl! She was pale and seemed familiar.

Nick shook his head coming back to the present. He was trembling, creeping out, running to find his best friends who were also his brother-in-law, and cousins. Instead, he found a police headquarter.

"I need help!" he addressed a cop at the station.

"Sir, please! Calm down," the cop said.

"My brother-in-law and cousins ... are gone ... vanished," Nick searched for words. His heart was pumping. He was breathless.

"Sir, come with me!" the cop gave him water and sat him in a room. He then called the sheriff.

"Where are your friends, Mr. Nick?" Sheriff Anderson kept interrogating.

What happened there was inexplicable. Nick was speechless. He was in extreme shock.

"We want to find your friends. But if you won't cooperate, we are helpless," the cop said.

Nick did too! But what to tell them: a vortex swallowed his friends in an ordinary forest during a normal camping trip? But he has to tell someone before his heart burst. Nick had no choice but to tell as it happened.

"You mean to say that an unusual ditch, gulped three full grown men, mystically," Sheriff Anderson was suspicious and furious with this insane theory. "Is this some kind of practical joke? If it is … I assure you, Mr. Nick, it's not funny!"

"We are losing our patience!" the cop hit on the table.

"No. Please … help me!"

"For crying out loud, last time, where are your friends? What did you do to them?" the cop inquired, one last time.

"I swear! I did not do it! The spirit in me forced me," Nick was frantic.

The police had to call in a psychiatrist to find out Nick's state of mind. After talking to Nick for two hours, the psychiatrist concluded, Nick was mentally unstable.

"I am not crazy! My friends are in the forest!" Nick was shouting at the top of his lungs.

Sheriff Anderson ordered a search. Relatives were informed. They came to help police in the search for their loved ones. Some relatives stayed with Nick. All were connected to each other. Everyone was sad for the victims and Nick as well. Detectives were called. It was a huge case, now.

"There's no sign of *any* forest. And if there's no forest, then there's no ditch! Any logical explanation?" confused detective discussed with the team.

"Nick, please help us understand!" the detective asked, impatiently. "Do you need a lawyer?"

"No," Nick was looking at the floor. His tears had stopped. His energy and will was broken. Now even he doubted himself of being mentally stable.

Nick was convicted but sent to a mental institute instead, due to his psychosis.

His sisters and mother were left alone. Family and friends were mourning all four. They were not bitter with Nick but confused and terribly shattered. They fought for his release.

But before any action could take place, Nick mysteriously disappeared. According to the ward nurse and other hospital witnesses, Nick was hallucinating. He kept saying that, a 13-year-old girl is coming soon to take him to the ditch, to meet his friends.

The movie playing out in front of me, ended. I was tearful!

"What was ... that?" I could barely speak. "What did you ... do to me?"

"It was the truth!" Lizzy said in a loud voice.

"Okay. Tell me, *who* were they? *Why* did you show me that? And how?"

"Why ...?" she paused then said the words I never wanted to hear. "Ask your MOTHER!"

I ran as fast as I could. I wanted to get away before she hurt me. I kept thinking. *What does my Mom have to do with it? Who were they? Why is all this happening to me?*

My brain was mystified.

CHAPTER VII

... OTHER ALANA

"Coming, *coming*," Mom opened the door.

I forced my way in.

"Baby what's wrong? Calm down! Why are you gasping?" Mom stroked my back.

"Mom ... I need to talk!" I controlled my breath and pulled her hand into my room.

"Honey, you are worrying me! Where were you?" Mom was concerned.

"Is everyone asleep?" I asked because I needed her total attention and I didn't want to worry my little sister.

"Yes they are. You are worrying me, Alana!" Mom said. "Did your friend do something?"

"Yes and no!" I replied. "Mom ... she's weird. She told me something and I don't know what to make of it?"

"What did she tell you, Alana?" Mom was extremely concerned.

I told her from A to Z, everything I saw — each of their names, and what heartbreak struck them. Mom had tears in her sad eyes. She was rubbing her hands together. I had a feeling — she's about to tell me a terrible secret that I was unaware of, for so many years.

"Nick was my older brother," she was quiet again.

I didn't know Mom had a brother, and I just witnessed what had happened to my *uncle*. I had my hand on my mouth in shock.

"Demitry was our soon to be brother-in-law. Rob and Murray were our first cousins," Mom continued in a faint voice. "We were more than just relatives—we were best friends. Your Aunt Jill knew Demitry since kindergarten. They got engaged when they were in college. All five of us were barely apart from each other's lives. If one of us was in trouble, we were all there for him. I was the youngest and spoiled by all five. At the time of the incident I was six," she took a deep breath then started again, "Jill and I were supposed to go on that trip, too. But Mother said I was too young. So Jill didn't go as well, to make me happy. Jill never got married, and we never stopped searching for four of them," Mom paused to wipe her tears.

I didn't know what to say? I hugged her.

She continued, "Our ancestors believed — it has something to do with your Great Grandmother, Alana. She and her middle school friend–I don't know her name–they used to play in an abandoned, wrecked house near the forest. One day, they were playing as usual but they decided to go explore the forest. Alana came back but her friend was never found. Not even her body. Alana told that she last saw her in the forest. The police doubted Alana because she was the last one to see her. But that friend's aunt and uncle never doubted Alana because she was devoted to find their niece and her best friend. When Alana grew up and got married, nothing went perfectly in her life: her husband died just after six years of their marriage; three of her daughters died at a young age due to unusual diseases and cause — like one of them died playing marbles with friends, near the forest. Only your Grandfather survived, somehow,"

"You need water, Mom," I asked.

"I'm fine, Honey. Are you sure, you want to hear more?" Mom was worried for me.

"I definitely need some answers, Mom," I told her.

"Okay then," Mom said. "When Alana died due to old age, her maid found a letter under her pillow. She Wrote:

'I am sorry for the heartache I caused because of jealousy. May our future generations, be save of this curse that I brought upon us. Bestow one of my great-granddaughters with my name to keep me blissful.'

The maid gave the letter to Alana's siblings. They saved it for future generations — to guide them to stay safe and stay away from any wrong doing. It still exists in our family," And he wanted to fulfill his Mother's wish by giving you, her great-granddaughter, the name, Alana. So I agreed to honor her wish," Mom gasped as if she was relieved from a burden of secrecy.

But there was much more she wanted to share with me. "When I was younger, I kept dreaming of getting lost in a dark forest and looking into a ditch, full of darkness. My Dad gave me a flashlight on my seventh birthday saying, 'It will keep you safe, sweetie. Use it only when you truly need it,' I never understood what that meant but I always kept it with me until I passed it on to you, when you started having the same dreams. But I'm sorry I never told you this because I thought the dreams are not a curse but just a coincidence and it'll stop, soon. My dreams stopped when I got married."

"It's okay, Mom. I know you wanted to keep me away from all this," I hugged her.

And then Mom raised a question that made me think, too. "Not even your Dad knows about *all* this, how does your friend know? Who is *this* Lizzy?" Mom was worried.

"I don't know, Mom. For sure, she's *not* a friend. But I'm going to find out!" I assured her.

"No, you won't, Alana! Keep away from her. I'm telling John everything, first thing in the morning," she decided.

"But Mom," I said.

"You are not sleeping alone, tonight. Come to our room. I'll bring Melody from her room, too,"

Mom said.

I couldn't sleep. My brain was searching for solutions. Then I made the silliest decision *ever* — I had to free my family and future generations, from this curse — once and for all. It was silly because I had no idea where to start? What is in store for me, and how do I get rid of this curse? I had to find answers.

The next morning, I heard mom say, "Let's go. We have to get there soon, so we can get familiar with each corner of the house, during daylight because there is no electricity right now.

"We have to use candles and lanterns just for a day or two. And for cooking, we can do barbeque or order out," Dadum said.

"Mom," I whispered, "did you tell Dadum … *the secret?*

"I don't want to worry him during moving. I promise I'll tell him in our new home. Don't worry, Alana. After moving you'll be away from that girl. Everything will be fine ... I promise!" she whispered. "Are you okay, Alana?" Mom asked again.

"I'm fine. Just starving," I didn't want to worry her so I didn't let her know that after last night, I will not be the *same* Alana. I knew a secret that has no conclusion until I find all the answers, and a way to end it somehow.

"We'll get something on our way," Mom smiled because she barely lets us eat fast food — as I explained earlier.

The driver was ready — we got in the car, and left.

CHAPTER VIII

THE MOVE

When we got there — I saw the house and screamed — not with happiness but terror. The house was under some rotten trees, hanging over the roof; the inside was just normal; may I add — really normal — a huge house but not as I dreamt. I wanted to see all the stuff I liked — a big swing set in the patio; a spiral staircase going to my room; crystal chandelier in the foyer, and an extra room for my *collection*. Yup, I love collecting unique and extraordinary stuff. I have a huge collection of unique, adventurous knick knacks from our trips to amazing cities from the seven continents. I have cool spy gadgets from our trips to Europe and unique flashlights from Asia. I have wooden tools and jewelry from South America. I also collected bizarre, lucky charms and from Africa.

Yup, we travel *a lot!* We are an adventurous family but nothing was adventurous about this house.

Suddenly I saw someone. "Hey! Who is this young fellow?" I asked the real estate agent, Mrs. Greene.

"It's Ziv. He's my handsome dog," Mrs. Greene patted the dog's head.

Melody pulled Dadum's shirt and randomly begged. "Can we keep him, Daddy? Please, please, pretty please!"

"It's somebody's dog! You can't just take away someone's pet, silly!" I explained.

"I *can* let you keep it for a *while*!" Mrs. Greene offered.

She was a kind, gentle lady. But we don't need a dog!

"For real?" Melody said surprisingly.

"You certainly can, adorable!" she gave Melody's cheek a pinch as if she's the cutest thing in the World — which she really is. I love my sister but not in times when she doesn't make any sense. Melody is truly smart, especially in Mathematics — just like me.

"But ask your parents first! I mean it'll take *at least* two days for the security system to be installed. So my Ziv can be a guard dog!" Mrs. Greene added.

"You're too kind, we'll be fine!" Dadum replied.

"Please Dadum, please!" Melody begged by stealing *my* given nickname for Dad.

Mom signaled Dadum with her eyes. "A day won't hurt!" she always does that when she can't discuss in front of someone.

Dadum stroked the dog. "Well, okay then! Ziv is our guest for the night!"

I was beginning to like the idea of a pet for a day — no responsibility, just enjoy and return it to the rightful owner.

Oh well, Ziv is here; now let's continue with my tour. The inside and front was not worth looking; let's hope the backyard is worth living. I was being optimistic — kind of. But soon I was pessimistic. It was a big, old backyard with no blooming flowers. Mrs. Greene did not show us a house that's green. The grass was yellowish brown. *It's not that bad. At least it has a broken fountain in the middle of nowhere!* I thought.

But the worst was about to appear. As I was exploring the neighborhood, I noticed — there were no houses in sight. It was like our house was in a jungle — no scenic or cherishing views.

Oh, no! I gasped as I saw the worst thing yet. A CEMETERY, few yards away from our house! Some of the engraved names were of people who died just a few days ago, which made me *more* sad. Why did we buy this house? I doubt anyone ever lived in this house. This was definitely not how I imagined our house would be. It was getting late. As I walked back, on the faded pathway and dead leaves, I overheard someone talking in a ghostly voice. They were chanting my name, *ALANA*, again and again with no sudden pause. I felt goosebumps.

Suddenly, it struck me: our house was at that same place—I followed Lizzy that unforgettable night. The same cemetery, someone chanting my name, weird trees ... it is that place! How is this possible? Is it written in my fate to be here? Is this place connected with our family secret?

I decided to go find out what was happening. I went in the house, packed my adventure bag with all the tools I needed, and left. I didn't want to but, they are chanting *my* name, so it is kind of *my* business. I have to find out who is that and why are they calling out my name?

"Mom, I'll be back. I'm not going far. Okay?"

"Be back before its dark. And take Ziv with you for protection," Mom said while unpacking.

I took Ziv. We walked pass the cemetery.

Oh please be any neighbors. I was praying for some friends.

"O' Ziv, it wouldn't be creepy if we had population!"

All of a sudden Ziv barked at something! I turned around to see who he was barking at. I nearly jumped out of my skin when I saw her standing under a tree. "It's *not* possible!" I whispered.

"What's not possible?" she heard me whispering.

"How did you …"

"Find you?" she interrupted. "You are my best friend, Alana! I can't leave you," Lizzy said, wickedly.

I pulled Ziv's leash and ran. Ziv kept barking. I looked back, she was not there. But I didn't slow down. As I reached the porch, I saw her sitting there on the stairs. My mouth was wide open with fear and shock.

"How did …? You?" I babbled.

"I will not leave you alone until you know the whole truth!" she said.

Ziv was barking constantly. I pulled my thoughts together and took Ziv's leash to put him inside the house, then finally said, "Leave me alone, whoever or whatever you are! My Mother told me about the curse. What do you have to do with it? Give me answers or leave!" I was furious and once again, baffled about her sudden entrances.

"You will find out *very* soon," she replied slyly and disappeared in thin air.

It was not shocking anymore. Weird things happening, was like a routine now.

The chanting started once again—*Alana*, AL-ANA. I was ready to face whoever it was. *Here I come!* I have to figure things out if I want to live peacefully every again.

CHAPTER IX

FINDING OUT

I went inside. Everyone was busy. I sneaked into my room upstairs—found my suitcase and took out my treasured flashlight. I'm going to take it with me. When my mother gave it to me on my seventh birthday, she told me—the flashlight will keep me safe. I never knew what she meant and when to use it. But I truly believed in it anyway. And now I know my mother believes in it more than me.

Once again I was ready to face Lizzy. I left the

house following the chant. It was growing louder and louder. And as it was getting near, I was getting impatient but not scared at all. It's my destiny.

As I walked deeper in the forest I saw a bright light. It felt like my eyes were going to get blind.

"There you are!" my forehead wrinkled — my eyebrows curved with rage.

I saw Lizzy floating in the bright light but with no shadow. She was the one reciting my name. "I knew it!" my doubt was positive.

But this time, I could hear the whole thing:

"Lizzy, I will take the revenge. Oh, Alana … you are such a good friend. Take revenge from the other Alana. Alana you can do it. Alana is back!"

What does she mean by that? As my mind raced

ahead it put all the clues together and I was positive that she's a ghost. But why the name Lizzy sounded so familiar. I've definitely heard it a long time ago.

I jumped out of hiding. "Hey!" I confronted her. "I know you are a ghost, Lizzy."

She came down on the ground. "Ghost? Tsk, tsk! I prefer the term— spirit," she beamed.

She was coming near me.

I backed up a little. "That's hilarious. I believe spirits are the respectful ones. And you are nothing but a demonic manifestation of some Lizzy girl," I was intimidated by her creepy looks but retained my courage to finally face her about the truth. I started walking around her. "What I don't get is that—what do you have to do with our *family secret?* Do you have something to do with my Great-Grandmother? If yes, why am I the target?"

"You are quite close, Alana. But not close enough," she looked into my eyes seriously. "First you have to remember the whole story, Alana. Then I can kill you," she held my shoulders tighter and kept staring into my eyes.

I felt like I was being hypnotized. I tried to look away with all my power but it was too late. I fainted on the ground, and soon I was dreaming. Once again it didn't seem like a vision but a television — everything happening right in front of me:

"Oh, I just don't like *Lizzy*," Alana said making faces. "She is so rich and always the best student in the school. She has a great big house, and mine is pathetic. What a pity!" Alana told Billy with jealousy.

Alana was angry with the city girl, Lizzy, since she arrived to their serene, country high school:

"Hello, I'm Lizzy," she said to Julie, one of her classmates.

But before Julie could reply, Alana who was standing right beside Julie, interrupted, "We don't say *hello* to a complete stranger who is not familiar with our rules and regulations. When you learn, then come and say hi!"

"Oh. Okay. When do I get started? I'm a fast learner and a very intelligent student," Lizzy said without getting bullied by Alana's rudeness.

"Wow," Julie was impressed by Lizzy. "Welcome to 'Humble High!" Julie shook hands with Lizzy but Alana did not and just walked away.

Alana's jealousy increased when Billy started favoring Lizzy. "You have to give her a chance, Al. I think she's sweet. Maybe she's not as bad as you might think."

"How many times do I have to tell you, don't call me Al!" Alana was furious.

"Okay. Calm down. You know what, Alana? You are a changed person after Lizzy's arrival," Billy walked away.

"Hmph. Whatever, Lizzy's pet," Alana didn't care.

Day by day, Lizzy was getting praise from the teachers for being respectful and sophisticated. Lizzy was a gentle, loving soul. She was not interested in going to parties and wasting time. But she was in need of a best friend. She had Billy and Julie, but she wanted Alana's friendship. Lizzy liked Alana because of her funky, carefree nature.

On the other hand, Alana was planning to embarrass or outcast Lizzy somehow.

"Hi, Alana. What are you doing here?" Lizzy said just to make a conversation.

Alana wanted to say: can't you see dummy, it's a library and what do people do at a library? But then her revengeful mind gave her a clever idea of being close to Lizzy and finding out more about her. Then it'll be much easier to humiliate her. "Oh, hi!" Alana beamed. "I'm borrowing a book for an essay."

"I wanted to ... um ... ask you if you ... I mean ... we can forget about our first meeting and be ..." Lizzy hesitated.

"Be pals?" Alana finished Lizzy's sentence impatiently.

Both laughed.

Next couple of weeks; it was their routine to

meet at each other's house or at the abandoned house near a vast forest, not too far from Alana's house. It was a creepy but a quiet place for friends to chat. Sometimes Billy and Julie would tag along with them. They were happy of Lizzy and Alana's friendship. But no one knew that Alana was just acting to be a friend.

On the weekend they went to Julie's party. Usually Lizzy stays away from parties but Alana convinced her to go. "It's splendid. Julie throws the greatest parties. You have to come!" Alana thought this was the perfect opportunity to humiliate her in front of everyone.

But at the party, Lizzy started admiring her. "You are so nice, Alana! I wanted to be your friend because you don't take life *too* seriously. Other students treat me as a science nerd; teachers treat me as the future *Einstein*. But you treat me as a normal teenager."

So Alana postponed her plot for the day, thinking maybe her jealousy is not worth it.

"You know why we moved here?" Lizzy shared.

"No idea!" Alana replied in her usual careless way.

"I'm an orphan and I used to live in a foster home."

"You? Um ... an orphan? I had no idea," Alana was surprised.

"They treated every kid as worthless beings. I was smart from the beginning. I knew I could *never* succeed while living here. So I ran away in search for my birth parents," Lizzy's head was down.

"Really?" Alana choked up.

"No silly! Not really!" Humor shined in Lizzy's face. Her laughter was friendly and harmless.

But Alana didn't think it was funny. She felt Lizzy treated her as a stupid person who fell for it.

"Okay. Enough jokes. I'm not an orphan but my Father left us when I was one and I never really knew him. Then my Mama didn't want to raise me, so she left me with her sister, Josephine, and married some rich guy. They never checked up on me ever again. But Aunt Josephine and Uncle Floyd gave me so much affection and care; I don't miss my real parents or even think about them." Lizzy said.

"Are you telling the truth this time," Alana asked.

"Yes," Lizzy replied truthfully.

Even though Lizzy was telling the truth Alana didn't care. "Yeah right," she said and left.

One day Lizzy shared her thoughtful opinion about Alana's grades. "Yesterday Billy was saying, your grades were not that bad in elementary!"

"What?" Alana's eyebrows rose. "When did this happen?" Alana was desperately curious.

"I told you, silly — yesterday after Julie and you went to the fair." Lizzy was totally frank with her best friend. But Lizzy was unaware that she was feeding Alana's anger more and more each day.

"Why does Billy care and more importantly, why do you care?" Alana exclaimed, rudely."

"Isn't he your best friend since kindergarten? And I'm your brand *new* friend — so we want to help you succeed," Lizzy tried to cheer her up.

"I don't need any help! Especially from you, LIZZY!" Alana gave Lizzy
a hard, unblinking stare and walked away.

"That's it. I can't pretend anymore," Alana
was talking to herself in the school mirror. "I have
an idea. I'll take her to the weird forest and try to
scare her a bit. That'll teach her a lesson!" Alana
walked down to Lizzy's house — knocked on the
door. Lizzy came out.

"Hi Lizzy. Do you want to come explore the
woods and chat?" Alana asked politely.

"Um ... I don't know? We've never been there,"
Lizzy was not sure. "I remember Billy saying something about the forest being eerie."

"Ha ... are you a scaredy cat," Alana teased.

"Am not! Oh, alright," Lizzy smiled not

knowing what's in store for her.

Both walked in the woods and finally reached the one place, they should have never crossed.

"Come on! Catch me, slow tiger!" Alana kept going deeper in the woods to find a perfect place to leave Lizzy alone and run away.

"Alana, please don't go any farther. I admit it. I am scared of this forest," Lizzy was hysterical trying to find Alana. Lizzy had no choice but to follow to keep her silly friend safe. While Lizzy was running, she had a bad feeling something was going to happen. But she didn't stop; she kept on running to find Alana. But then Lizzy's fear became a truth—Lizzy tripped, and fell in a deep pit which was hidden from yellow leaves. She never knew the ditch was there.

Right then Alana turned around and couldn't

see Lizzy, so she went back, thinking—that's
enough torture for today.

"Hey, Lizzy! Give up?" Alana shouted while
going back. "Yoo-hoo! Oh, so now you're trying
to scare me … the champion of pranks!" Alana
couldn't find Lizzy so she assumed that, Lizzy is
hiding to scare her.

"What is this?" Alana came near the ditch.
"Couldn't be?" she convinced herself that Lizzy
couldn't have fallen into this. She has two eyes.
"Lizzy it's not funny anymore!" Alana said.
"LIZZY!" she kept shouting for hours—looking
in the ditch—running around, but Lizzy did not
reply back.

But Lizzy was long gone—killed this unfaith-
ful day, in the ditch of death. Lizzy never thought
that the best friend she trusted will be the reason
of ending her life.

"I didn't want this to happen at all," Alana had a change of heart. She feared the worst. Her heartbeat was thundering. She tried to calm herself. "I know Lizzy went back home. She's not lost. Maybe she's trying to fool me," Alana tried to be optimistic and decided to go to Lizzy house and catch her there.

Alana knocked on Lizzy's door. "Aunt Josephine, is Lizzy home?" Alana asked as if nothing happened and also reassuring herself that Lizzy came back home.

"No dear, she is not home. Check with Billy or Julie. She was planning to go on a secret mission with them. That silly girl!" Aunt Josephine said, smiling.

Alana left — went home and didn't share with anyone.

The next morning, Alana woke up from the noise of chaos. She looked out of her window and saw — her parents and a few neighbors from around the block, worried and giving directions.

"You go at the top side of the Mountain Arama," the senior neighbor ordered.

Alana got dressed and went down to see what's all the hubbub? But deeply she knew what was going on?

"What is going on, Mama?" Alana asked her worried mother.

"Um ... sweetie ... go back in. Nothing is wrong," Mama hid the facts.

"Is Lizzy fine?" Alana felt guilty. She wanted to find Lizzy.

"How did you ... um ... yes it is about Lizzy," Mama hesitated but told her. "Lizzy's Aunt said she didn't come home last night."

"I want to find her, Mama. Can I search too?" Alana wanted to make everything back to normal.

"No dear. We don't know yet—who took her? Is she really missing? What happened? There can be a criminal on the loose," Mama said.

"No, there isn't," Alana wanted to tell everything but paused. "I mean ... uh ... everyone is good here. No bad people."

"Okay, then. But don't go alone. Go with your father," Mama said.

Alana's father was talking to neighbors.

"Daddy!" Alana wanted her father's attention.

"What is it, Alana?" he turned around.

"I think we should go look at the forest," she couldn't hide anymore.

"We already looked there," he said.

"But you didn't look near the ditch. Did you?" she questioned.

"What ditch?" Daddy was puzzled.

"Daddy ... I went with Lizzy to the forest, yesterday but I could not find her afterwards. I think she fell. But I never saw her falling or anything," Alana burst into tears.

"Oh, Alana! Why didn't you tell us?" Daddy was concerned. "It is okay. We *will* all go now. I will go tell Lizzy's Aunt and Uncle. We will find her," he calmed Alana.

Alana, Daddy, Uncle Floyd and a few others went to the ditch.

Firefighters were called. They went down the ditch. Alana's fingers were crossed. She forgot all about her jealousy. But it was too late. The firefighters came out empty handed. Lizzy was not there. The search continued around the forest and town.

After months of dedicated search, Lizzy's beloved Aunt and Uncle decided to arrange a funeral. Other relatives and town's people agreed to bury an empty casket to make her soul rest in peace.

Alana was against it. She wanted to keep searching. "We can't give up now. Lizzy must be waiting for us."

"It's okay, Alana. Thank you for caring!" Aunt Josephine said in a broken, sobbing voice. "Lizzy's at a better place now. She must be looking over you, proudly, that you cared."

Alana thought — *no she's not proud but furious — I'm the reason she's gone. Don't thank me I took your precious away from you. I will never rest in peace.*

At the funeral, Billy told Alana, "A few days before her disappearance, she decided to give you a surprise birthday party," Billy choked up. "Lizzy called it a secret mission," he hugged Alana. "I thought you should know this, about your best friend."

Alana froze with grief; she was truly remorseful. Her heart broke into millions of pieces. Alana's life will never be the same.

"I killed her!" she shouted inside the closed doors of her room.

"I ... I killed her!" I saw the truth. "It was I who killed her ..."

Lizzy interrupted, screaming, "YES YOU DID, ALANA!"

It was all clear to me. "It was my past life. And Lizzy died because of me," tears came out of my eyes.

"I waited so long for you to be reborn. Until then, I took few useless lives," Lizzy made a disgusted face.

"Now that you are reincarnated, I can take revenge from the real guilty person!"

At last, I remembered who she was and that's why her name was so familiar. "I'm sorry, Lizzy!" I recognized her from my past life. She was friend, Lizzy. "I dragged you towards your untimely death."

I realized it wasn't her fault that she wants revenge. "You've waited long enough. I know you want to kill me, Lizzy. But I'm not ruthless in this life—I care, I am a kind hearted person. I would never dare to end someone's precious life. Try to understand, Lizzy!" I wanted her to realize, and move on.

"Lizzy, *Lizzy, Lizzy!* Why do you keep calling me that?" she bristled, enraged with me.

"That's your name. You are Lizzy. Aren't you?" I asked.

"You still don't get it. Do you?" Lizzy appeared right in front of me. "Look at *me*. You know who *I am!* Remember what you promised while on your deathbed. Remember?"

"Ahhh!" I shouted frustratingly. "What? Tell me, already!"

"You promised to take revenge for Lizzy's sake. You promised to kill Alana if she's ever born again," she touched my shoulders. "I'm fulfilling your dying wish," her face turned exactly like mine. It was like I was looking at a mirror.

"What the ..." I stepped back, stumbling over my feet in shock.

"Do you get it now? I'm not Lizzy, I am YOU! I'm ALANA," she ground her teeth in rage.

"So let me get it straight ... you are saying that you are PAST me? Then what happened to Lizzy?" I asked the past Alana.

"Lizzy never came back from the ditch. She must be in Heaven. I disguised myself as Lizzy because she deserves to live in everyone's eyes ... *not* Alana," she told me, angrily. "Don't you remember the past life promise you made to yourself: if Alana is ever reborn, you will kill her — to keep everyone safe from your cruel nature. And you left a letter of warning, as well," she reminded me. "But the letter couldn't save anyone. You started targeting: You appeared as Lizzy, and captured Nick's soul, and made him push Rob, Demitry and Murray in the ditch. Later, you took Nick from the hospital to the *Famished Forest* and pushed him too," *past* Alana told *present* Alana.

"But wait … how did Great-Grandmother's children die mysteriously? Did she kill them?" I was perplexed.

She corrected me. "Not Great-Grandmother's kids … you mean, your kids, Alana."

"Whatever," I said.

She continued. "No you didn't kill them. They were killed because of your deeds. It was your fate to suffer the loss of your loved ones — to feel Lizzy's aunt and uncle's loss."

She made me feel guilty for destroying so many lives. I fell for it. But luckily, I controlled my state of mind. "Stop it! Stop judging me! Stop saying I did all this. It was YOU, my past life, which I'm truly sorry for. But now I care about this life — the deeds of this life. And in this life, I can never hurt, even an ant!" I pushed her. "So get out of my life, Alana — let me live peacefully."

"It's not that easy, *present* Alana," she pushed me back scornfully.

CHAPTER X

COME WITH ME

"Now stop being a baby, and get ready to fall in the ditch," her voice became chilling.

But I didn't fall for her terror — not anymore. "Too bad Alana, you can't justify your crimes by saying, you are doing this for Lizzy," I made her realize. "Lizzy is definitely in a better place. That's why her spirit never came back for revenge. You are doing all this just for your own happiness."

"You can never understand what I did is blameless. My purpose has to end with you. Alana, you have to die!" she said and flew near me — grabbed my left hand, and started chugging.

Now was the time to save myself. I took out the flashlight from my shoulder bag — faced it towards her, and turned it on. As the light flashed on her, she screamed like an animal. I got a chance to run away. I shook my hand to free from her grip and ran opposite direction. As I was running, I looked down at the flashlight. Some words appeared — it read:

"Find Famished Forest!"

Alana was running hastily to catch me. I was looking here and there, desperate to find a forest, particularly named, *Famished*.

"Oh no!" I stopped with a sudden brake as the trees started rising up from the ground, out of

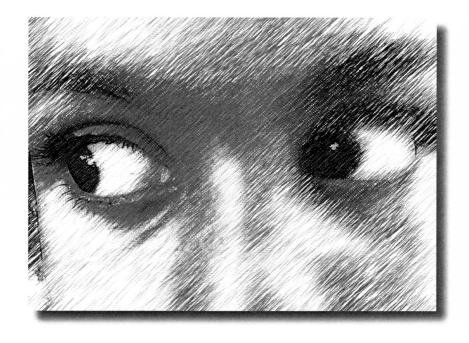

nowhere. In just a few seconds, there was a wide-spread forest in front of me. I didn't know what to do next. She almost caught up with me. So I ran into the forest. I kept going, until I found any sign. I took a second look at the flashlight. It read:

"This Should End in the Ditch!"

"Please be there, please!" I tried to remember the exact location of the ditch, in which Lizzy fell, an era ago. I remember the ditch was near yellow, burnt grass.

There it was! I stopped running.

"Come on; run fast!" I looked back and shouted to trap Alana.

"I am right here!" Alana appeared behind Alana.

I shudder, but quickly used my mind and turned on the flashlight. She screamed and started walking backwards. I had her exactly where I wanted.

"Almost there," I said, looking at Alana, who was getting close to the pit.

"Fall, Alana, fall!" a roar mixed with tears came out of my shaky lips.

"I will come back for you, Alana!!" she screamed while falling in the deep, dark pit.

The ditch sealed and wiped out.

I fell down on my knees; hid my face into my hands. I managed to put myself together. As I looked up, the forest was gone, along with the ditch.

CHAPTER XI

THE FINISH

At last, the chapter of *the ... other Alana* was over. I started walking with heavy feet but free heart.

As I reached my home, these words came out of my mouth, "Wow!" My mouth was wide open. "Is that my house?"

The trees hanging over the house weren't rotten anymore. They were beautiful; it was a great sight. Pink, purple and even blue flowers grew *everywhere*. The mansion was a turquoise, two-floored house. I walked in and saw a crystal chandelier sparkling in the foyer. Lights were on. We had electricity. It was like a cloud of darkness was lifted and I could see my real home — a beautiful, dream home.

"There you are! We are waiting for you!" Mom held my hand and took me to the dining room.

The dining table was filled with variety of foods: corn on the cob and hominy, gravy, cranberry sauce, bread rolls, yams, and a huge turkey in the middle.

"Happy Thanksgiving!" Melody jumped from her chair and came to hug me.

"Good Thanksgiving, Dear!" Dadum kissed my forehead.

I was confused. "Uh ... Thanksgiving?"

Mom smiled. "Did you forget it's Thanksgiving?"

"I sure did, Mom!" I hugged her tightly.

"Go, clean up," Mom said. "We'll wait for you."

"Come soon. I am starving," Melody ordered while rubbing her tummy.

I went upstairs to my room. Ziv followed me — barking and wagging.

Everything was just perfect! While cleaning up I thought, I would have my whole life to tell them the curse has been broken. But tonight I will just enjoy the greatest Thanksgiving, with my loving family.

"Let's start, Dadum!" I said.

My Dad always starts the prayer and then carves the turkey.

"How did you cook all this?" I asked Mom because we just moved.

"I have magic hands!" she twirled her fingers. "Okay, you caught me—I ordered take out."

"Mom? You?" at last, Mom is ordering from outside.

"I know. *I know*. But I had no options. And how can I ever let you guys go without a Thanksgiving dinner!" Mom explained.

Dinner was over. After helping with the dishes, I kissed my gentle Mom—my caring Dadum, and my cutest sister—and went to my room.

While sitting on my bed — I smiled, and looked at the flashlight, then closed my eyes and said, *"Another Adventure Awaits!"*

THE END

ABOUT THE AUTHOR

Aihber Khan lives in Florida with her family. She won her first award as a writer and illustrator in a National contest in 2008, when she was just six. The same year, Aihber was interviewed by *The Palm Beach Post*, for winning the contest, and for her educational achievement as a Gifted student. Besides writing, she plays chess, really loves singing and does karate. But most of all, she loves to have a valuable and fun filled time with her family.

Website: www.Aihber.com

Email: alanaandthe@aihber.com

Facebook: www.Facebook.com/Aihber

Youtube Channel: www.youtube.com/aihberkhan